Traduit par Nadège Verrier

© The Salariya Book Company Ltd, 1996.
Publié par Watts en 1996.
Titre original : *Medieval town*.
© Editions Epigones, 1997,
pour l'édition française.

ISBN 2-7366-4816-1
Dépôt légal : octobre 1997,
Bibliothèque nationale.
Imprimé par Eurografica.

Editions Epigones
80, rue de Vaugirard
75006 Paris

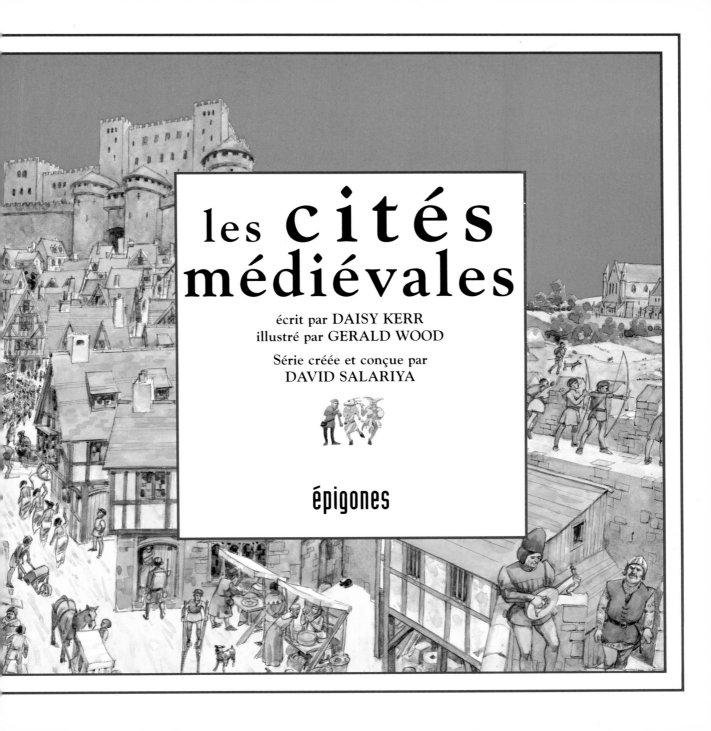

les cités médiévales

écrit par DAISY KERR
illustré par GERALD WOOD

Série créée et conçue par
DAVID SALARIYA

épigones

Au Moyen Âge

(entre le Ve et le XVe s.) la vie était essentiellement rurale même si les villes, centres de commerce et de défense, jouaient un rôle très important.

Bâties comme des forts, certaines des plus anciennes cités abritaient les soldats du roi et les dirigeants. D'autres étaient, à l'origine, d'anciens marchés locaux. Beaucoup de ces villes étaient relativement petites par rapport aux villes actuelles, comptant moins de 1000 habitants ; quelques-unes dépassaient néanmoins les 10 000 habitants.

Les gardes faisaient des rondes autour de la ville pour surveiller les étrangers. Dès la nuit tombée, les portes de la cité étaient fermées à clef. À l'intérieur de l'enceinte, des veilleurs patrouillaient toute la nuit, criant chaque heure.

Croix en or ou en argent

des églises, vêtements, bijoux et meubles des grandes maisons, soies et épices des entrepôts, sculptures et tapisseries des ateliers-boutiques des artisans et trésors de pièces des banques : toute cette concentration de richesses faisait des cités des cibles privilégiées.

Les villes étaient protégées par d'épaisses murailles et de robustes portes qui décourageaient l'ennemi et rendaient l'accès ou la fuite des voleurs plus difficile. Pour plus de sécurité, une douve remplie d'eau, un rempart de terre (la motte) et de profonds fossés ceinturaient la ville.

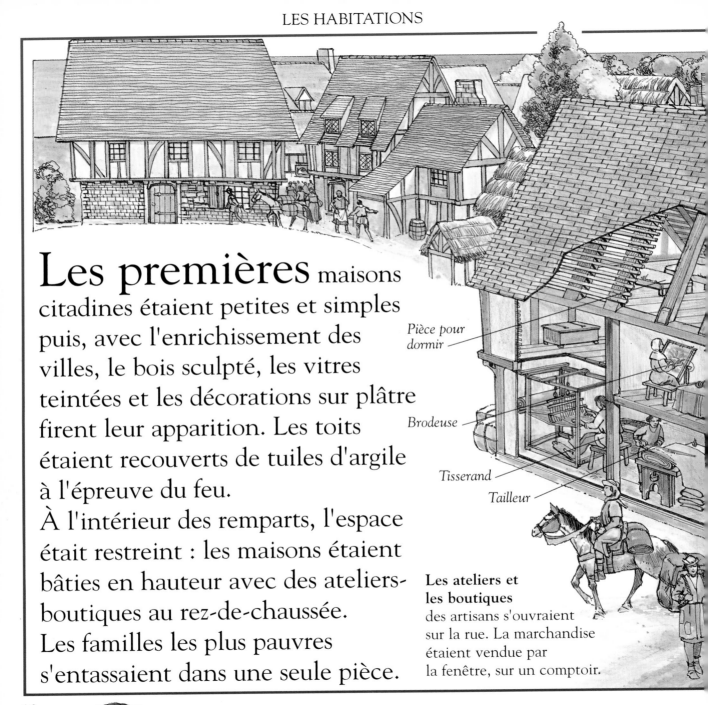

Les premières maisons

citadines étaient petites et simples puis, avec l'enrichissement des villes, le bois sculpté, les vitres teintées et les décorations sur plâtre firent leur apparition. Les toits étaient recouverts de tuiles d'argile à l'épreuve du feu.

À l'intérieur des remparts, l'espace était restreint : les maisons étaient bâties en hauteur avec des ateliers-boutiques au rez-de-chaussée. Les familles les plus pauvres s'entassaient dans une seule pièce.

Pièce pour dormir

Brodeuse

Tisserand

Tailleur

Les ateliers et les boutiques des artisans s'ouvraient sur la rue. La marchandise étaient vendue par la fenêtre, sur un comptoir.

Les paysans
amenaient
des troupeaux
de moutons pour
les vendre sur
le marché. Il existait des lois
pour garder les rues propres,
mais elles étaient souvent ignorées.

Tailleur de pierre

Vitrier

Charpentier

Tapissier

Tisserand

Fabricant de pièces

Orfèvre

Apprentis aidant un alchimiste dans ses expériences.

Les garçons (et quelques filles) apprenaient les métiers artisanaux en devenant apprentis. Vers l'âge de 8 ans, ils partaient vivre avec un maître et sa famille qui leur assuraient la nourriture, l'habillement, le logement et l'apprentissage du métier.

Au bout de 7 ans, les apprentis devenaient des « compagnons ». Les plus doués devaient réaliser une de leur spécialité (le « chef-d'œuvre ») qui était jugée par les jurés de la corporation. S'il était accepté, l'apprenti devenait maître à son tour.

Tondeur de moutons

Teinturier

Foulon

Fabricant de lanternes

Fabricant de dés

Bourrelier

Métallurgiste

Artiste

Sculpteur sur ivoire

Brodeuses

Souffleur de verre

Potier

Cordonnier

Forgeron

Au Moyen Âge, pratiquement tout était fait à la main. Les machines - tour de potier ou métier à tisser par exemple - étaient peu nombreuses et rudimentaires. Les artisans fabriquaient toutes sortes de biens, depuis les fins bijoux en or ou les vitres fragiles jusqu'aux aux lourds chaudrons de fer et aux épaisses bottes de cuir.

La plupart des marchands étaient installés en ville. Chaque profession avait sa corporation qui inspectait le travail, fixait les salaires et secourait les confrères malades.

Travailleur sur étain

Cloutier

Fabricant de bougies

Rémouleur

Tailleur

Armurier

Serrurier

Les marchands musulmans parcouraient l'Asie, l'Afrique du Nord et le Moyen-Orient, vendant des porcelaines de Chine et des poteries de Turquie et d'Iran (*à droite*).

Très bien armés, ces caravaniers du XIVᵉ s. traversaient le Sahara depuis le riche royaume du Mali. Leurs chameaux étaient chargés d'or.

Venise, ville marchande italienne, était un important centre commercial international.

Les marchandises les plus rares et les plus précieuses étaient vendues dans les boutiques. Les autres marchandises importées étaient vendues sur les étals des marchés.

On trouvait, à Venise, de la soie importée de Chine, des pierres précieuses d'Inde et du parfum d'Arabie.

Gingembre

Noix de muscade

Grains de poivre

Macis

Cardamome

Gousses de vanille

Importées d'Inde et des îles du Sud-Est asiatique, les épices étaient très prisées au Moyen Âge.

Certains marchands médiévaux voyageaient toute leur vie. Bravant les chemins montagneux escarpés, les immensités désertiques ou les mers démontées - sans compter la faim, le soleil et la maladie - ils rapportaient en Europe de précieuses marchandises venues d'Afrique, d'Asie, d'Inde et d'Orient. Quelles étaient leurs motivations ? Faire du commerce avant tout et pour certains, découvrir de nouveaux paysages et civilisations ou devenir riches.

Tournez la page pour découvrir le caravansérail

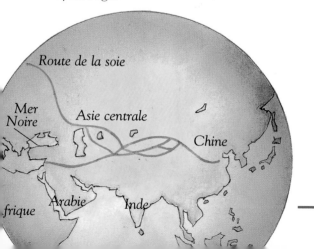

Route de la soie

Mer Noire

Asie centrale

Chine

Afrique Arabie Inde

La route de la soie était une voie commerciale traversant des contrées sauvages et dangereuses. Elle reliait la Chine à la mer Noire, en passant par l'Asie centrale. Les marchands de divers pays l'empruntaient pour acheter des produits qu'ils revendaient ensuite en ville.

Les bateaux déchargeaient sur les quais. Les autorités municipales percevaient les taxes et les droits de douane sur les marchandises importées.

Les villes
les plus importantes

et les plus prospères étaient bâties près de l'eau. À une époque où n'existaient ni camions, ni trains, ni avions, l'eau était le meilleur moyen de transporter les chargements lourds et volumineux. Les bateaux différaient selon leur usage. Les navires de guerre avaient, à chaque extrémité, des plates-formes servant aux combats. Les navires de commerce, eux, étaient dotés de larges et profondes coques pouvant transporter des cargaisons importantes.

Les traversées maritimes étaient très dangereuses. Les naufrages étaient fréquents de même que les attaques de pirates embusqués près des côtes.

Sur les mers du Nord, très venteuses, les navires étaient équipés de grandes voiles carrées dans lesquelles s'engouffrait le vent. En Méditerranée, la mer était beaucoup plus calme et les navires étaient propulsés par des avirons.

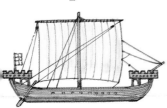

Navire de guerre du XIIIe s.

Bateau « rond » du XIIIe s.

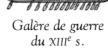

Cog de marchandises du XIVe s.

Galère de guerre du XIIIe s.

Caraque flamande du XVe s.

19

Pain

Étoffes

Oeufs

Dans la plupart des villes, le

marché se tenait au moins une fois par semaine. Dans les grandes cités, il était quotidien (à l'exception du dimanche). Les marchandises vendues - poisson, bétail, foin ou autres - étaient parfois présentées à des emplacements spécialisés. Les foires avaient lieu pendant les fêtes importantes, comme celle de Pâques.

Les marchandises étaient contrôlées pour vérifier leur qualité et leur valeur.

Poisson

Les grandes foires attiraient les marchands et les acheteurs de l'Europe entière. Il y avait des centaines d'étals, des spectacles et des tentes pouvant accueillir les visiteurs. Les conteurs, les acrobates, les chanteurs et les jongleurs divertissaient la foule.

À Noël, les momons revêtaient des masques animaliers et dansaient frénétiquement dans les rues de la ville en jouant de la musique.

Les membres des corporations de métiers jouaient des mystères, drames religieux relatant l'histoire sainte.

Les momons chantaient des chansons sur les légendes anciennes. La foule leur donnait de la nourriture ou de l'argent. Si elle ne le faisait pas, les momons la poursuivaient.

Mystère de la Nativité

Lors des festivals religieux importants, notamment celui de Pâques, les pièces de théâtre étaient données à l'intérieur des églises et des cathédrales. Les moines jouaient les moments importants de la vie de Jésus-Christ. Des chants et des cantiques chantés par le chœur étaient composés pour l'occasion.

C'est au Moyen Âge que furent joués les premiers mystères de la Nativité, racontant la naissance de Jésus.

Les momons jouaient de divers instruments de musique. De gauche à droite : viole, tambours, chalumeau, cornemuse, orgue de Barbarie, luth, double flûte.

En ville, les distractions étaient nombreuses.

Il y avait des défilés avec danses et musique, des pièces de théâtre, des spectacles de marionnettes et des chanteurs de rues. Les jours saints étaient chômés.

(Tournez la page pour découvrir la rue en fête).

Les bains publics ou les jardins privés permettaient de se détendre au calme. Après le travail, les hommes et les femmes allaient dans des tavernes pour discuter, boire de la bière, manger du pain et des pommes rôties et jouer aux dés ou aux cartes.

Le football était un sport très populaire, souvent aussi très violent. Il se jouait dans les rues, avec une vessie de porc en guise de ballon.

Vessie de porc

Les combats d'animaux étaient extrêmement violents. Ici, des chiens féroces sont lancés sur un ours attaché et muselé.

En ville, la nourriture était beaucoup plus variée qu'à la campagne. Sur le marché, on trouvait des fruits, des légumes, de la volaille, de la viande, du poisson mais aussi des aliments importés, comme le sucre, les dattes, le raisin et les épices. Il y avait des étals de pains et de gâteaux, des cabarets et des caves à vin. Dans les maisons des grandes cités, la viande était rôtie sur des feux ouverts et les pâtés étaient cuits dans des fours de briques.

On trouvait, dans la cuisine d'une famille riche, des œufs, des aromates, un lapin, des sacs de farine et des jarres de vin.

Le boulanger surpris à vendre du pain moisi était, en guise de punition, traîné à travers les rues de la ville.

Les plats chauds à emporter - pâtés de viande par exemple - étaient cuits dans des fours portables. Peu de gens avaient un four chez eux.

Il n'y avait pas de réfrigérateurs pour garder les aliments frais. Le poisson était séché, salé ou conservé dans du vinaigre.

Les chasseurs parcouraient les villes pour vendre les oiseaux, les lapins et les lièvres qu'ils avaient attrapés.

La nourriture des gens ordinaires était simple mais rassasiante, comme par exemple cette recette de potage de pois cassés :
1. Laissez tremper les pois secs une nuit entière.
2. Placez-les dans un récipient rempli d'eau, d'herbes, d'ail, d'oignons, de choux, d'un os de jambon ou de couenne de lard.
3. Laissez cuire lentement jusqu'à obtenir une soupe épaisse.
4. Servez avec du pain et du fromage.

Les repas étaient l'occasion de régaler les hôtes importants mais aussi de réunir la famille. Les enfants devaient avoir de bonnes manières à table.

USTENSILES DE CUISINE

1   2   3   4

1. Marmites
2. Cruche à eau
3. Couteaux
4. Pichets pour la bière

Coiffure
très travaillée

Capuchon

À la fin du XIVe s.,
les marchands,
les banquiers et
les citadins riches
portaient ce type
de vêtements.

Ce marchand
porte avec fierté
un porte-monnaie
rempli d'argent
accroché à
la ceinture.
Sa femme garde
son argent
en sécurité dans
les plis de sa robe
longue.

Chemise
à manches longues
que les femmes
portaient sous
leur robe longue.

Souliers
« à la poulaine »

Éperon

Porte-
monnaie

Vers 1450, s'habiller
était très
simple :
on mettait
d'abord une
chemise ample
(tunique)
puis des braies
de lin (culotte).
Ensuite venaient
les chausses (sorte
de jambières)
de laine.
Une braguette
ou brayette
(pan d'étoffe)
couvrait
l'espace entre les
deux jambières.
Enfin, on enfilait
un pourpoint
(veste sans
manche) et
lorsqu'il faisait
froid, un manteau.

Les prêtres, les moines
et les nonnes portaient
des robes de laine simples.

Les paysans et les gens ordinaires étaient vêtus d'habits robustes, simples et unis, faits de laine ou de toile filées à la maison. Ils étaient amples pour pouvoir travailler confortablement.

Les vêtements des plus riches pouvaient être très travaillés. Comme aujourd'hui, les modes passaient et changeaient. L'échantillon ci-dessus représente quelques-uns des habits, chapeaux, chaussures et bijoux portés par les riches citadins entre 1350 et 1450 environ.

Les habits
moyenâgeux coûtaient cher. Il fallait par exemple plusieurs mètres d'étoffe pour faire une robe longue et tous les vêtements étaient entièrement fabriqués à la main, depuis le filage et le tissage du fil jusqu'aux coutures.

Les citadins aimaient les beaux habits. Les riches marchands et leurs épouses portaient de longues robes de velours, doublées de fourrure et brodées de soie colorée et de véritables fils d'or.
Les enfants de familles riches portaient les mêmes habits que les adultes.
Les artisans portaient des tuniques robustes et des chausses de couleurs vives ; leurs femmes avaient des ceintures d'or ornées de joyaux.
Les pauvres faisaient eux-mêmes leurs vêtements ou les achetaient d'occasion.

Les cérémonies religieuses

jouaient un rôle important. Les citadins allaient à l'église au moins une fois par semaine, sans compter les cérémonies spéciales comme les mariages ou les enterrements.

Ils donnaient de l'argent à l'Église par œuvre de charité et pour la construction d'édifices majestueux. Les écoles et les collèges étaient dirigés par des prêtres et des moines.

Les pèlerins faisaient de longs voyages pour se recueillir auprès des sanctuaires (lieux de piété) des cités médiévales. Ils y achetaient des objets, comme la coquille ci-dessous, en souvenir.

Une cathédrale était une église spécifique, dirigée par un évêque. Celui-ci était responsable des églises de son évêché et devait veiller au comportement exemplaire de tous les prêtres, moines et nonnes sous son autorité.

Les splendides cathédrales érigées à la gloire de Dieu contribuaient au prestige des cités dans lesquelles elles étaient bâties.

On trouvait, dans la plupart

des villes du Moyen Âge, un très petit
nombre de riches et une masse
importante de pauvres. Les miséreux
étaient partout : mères et enfants
mendiant dans les caniveaux, hommes
à bout de forces recroquevillés sous
les porches ou réfugiés dans la paille
des étables et des arrière-cours.
Ces pauvres étaient, pour la plupart
d'entre eux, sans travail, trop faibles,
vieux ou malades. Au Moyen Âge,
les allocations ou les indemnités
n'existaient pas et sans le soutien
des amis ou de la famille, la mort
les guettait. Abandonnant
leur campagne, ils affluaient en ville
quémander de la nourriture ou
de l'argent aux plus riches.

La lèpre était si redoutée
que les malades étaient
contraints de porter
une crécelle pour
signaler leur arrivée.
Ils étaient souvent
jetés hors
de la ville.

La lèpre était
une maladie de peau
grave et contagieuse
qui entraînait
l'invalidité puis
la mort.

Beaucoup de pauvres
étaient parasités
par les poux, les puces
et les vers.

L'Église
apprenait aux
riches à partager
leurs richesses.
Rien n'était
immuable et
ils seraient
peut-être un jour
à la place
des pauvres.
Ce serait alors
leur tour
de mendier.

Les riches envoyaient
des servantes porter
des paniers de restes
aux portes de la ville
pour nourrir les plus
démunis.

*Les grandes cités
distribuaient
régulièrement du pain
aux mendiants
pendant les périodes
de disette.*

Cette carte (*à droite*), extraite d'un manuel de médecine du Moyen Âge, devait guider le médecin dans son étude des urines du patient en vue de déterminer la cause de sa maladie.

Les médecins pensaient que trop de sang était mauvais pour la santé. Avec des sangsues (vers suceurs), ils saignaient les malades.

Rares étaient les maisons équipées de toilettes. On utilisait un seau ou une fosse. Les autorités municipales demandaient aux gens de vider leurs déchets à l'extérieur de la cité.

La mortalité infantile

était très élevée dans les cités médiévales : près d'un enfant sur deux mourait avant l'âge de 5 ans, principalement victime de maladies. Les immondices jonchaient les rues et les voies d'eau, accélérant la reproduction des germes et des maladies. Les maisons et les boutiques surpeuplées contribuaient aussi à la rapide propagation de ces maladies.

Les magistrats municipaux (échevins ou consuls) essayaient d'apprendre aux habitants à garder leur environnement propre, sans beaucoup de succès.

Les hospices de Beaune,
en Bourgogne

Les nonnes
dirigeaient
de nombreux
hôpitaux. Les soins,
les médicaments
et la nourriture
étaient gratuits
pour les pauvres.

Malgré l'interdiction
de l'Église d'ouvrir
les corps des morts,
les médecins étudiaient
l'anatomie. Ces dessins
médiévaux représentent
un bébé dans le ventre
de sa mère.

La trépanation
(ouverture de la boîte
crânienne) était
supposée soigner
la folie, l'épilepsie et
les très fortes migraines.

La trépanation
était une opération
si dangereuse que
la plupart des malades
en mouraient !

Dentiste ou
arracheur de dents

À l'aide de
tenailles, le
dentiste arrachait
les dents pourries.
De l'alcool ou un
mélange d'herbes
permettait de
soulager la
douleur.

Sage-femme

Des sages-femmes
assistaient les femmes
qui accouchaient.
Les honoraires
des médecins étaient
trop chers pour
les gens du peuple.

La saignée
(ouverture d'une
veine pour faire
couler le sang) était
le traitement fréquent
(mais inefficace)
de bon nombre de
maladies courantes.

Entre 1347 et 1352,

la peste noire tua près de la moitié des Européens. Elle se traduisait par des grosseurs noirâtres douloureuses sous les bras et une très forte fièvre. L'épidémie fut particulièrement meurtrière dans les cités où les médecins assistaient, impuissants, à sa propagation. Les morts étaient enterrés à la hâte dans des fosses mais bien souvent les prêtres et les fossoyeurs tombaient malades et mouraient à leur tour.

La peste noire se transmet par la puce du rat qui, en piquant l'homme, inocule le bacille mortel dans son sang.

Les flagellants - pénitents - pensaient que la peste était un châtiment de Dieu pour les punir de leurs péchés. Ils se fouettaient en guise de repentir.

Puce

MOTS UTILES

Alchimiste : scientifique du Moyen Âge qui étudiait aussi la magie. Les alchimistes essayaient de trouver la formule permettant de changer le métal ordinaire en or.

Braguette : pièce d'étoffe fermant, en haut, les deux jambes d'une paire de chausses.

Compagnon : artisan qui n'est plus apprenti mais pas encore maître.

Corporation : association d'artisans du même métier.

Épilepsie : affection pouvant provoquer des convulsions.

Étain : métal argenté utilisé dans la fabrication des plats et des chopes.

Foulon : ouvrier travaillant une laine fraîchement tissée.

Lèpre : affection grave de la peau qui entraîne la chute des doigts, des orteils, etc... Il existe aujourd'hui un traitement.

Momons : gens du peuple qui, déguisés en animaux et parés d'un masque, dansaient et chantaient dans les rues.

Mystère : drame religieux joué par les membres des corporations.

Peste noire : maladie infectieuse mortelle propagée par la puce du rat.

Pilori : poteau en bois sur lequel les petits voleurs étaient exposés, bras et tête attachés, en signe de punition.

Sangsues : vers aquatiques suçant le sang.

Tapisserie : tableau tissé avec de la laine.

Tondeur de moutons : personne qui tondait la laine des moutons.

Trépanation : ouverture pratiquée dans la boîte crânienne pour soigner certaines maladies.

Eyewitness
SKELETON

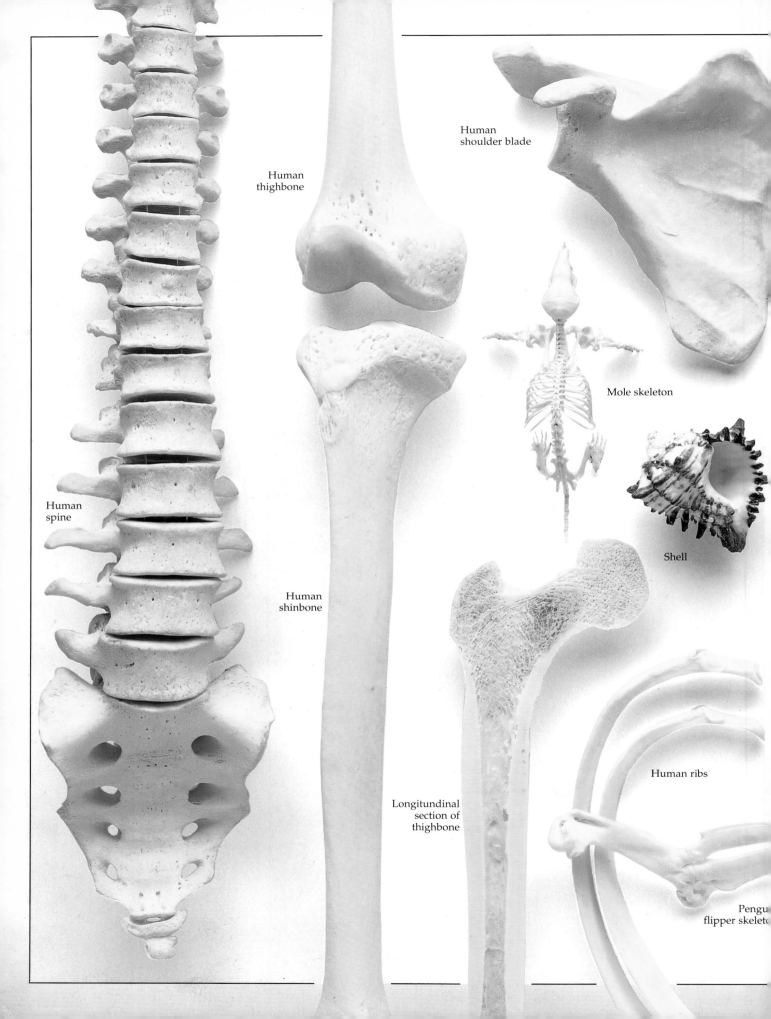

Human
thighbone

Human
shoulder blade

Mole skeleton

Human
spine

Shell

Human
shinbone

Human ribs

Longitundinal
section of
thighbone

Pengu
flipper skeleto

Human molars

Star shell

Eyewitness
SKELETON

Written by
STEVE PARKER

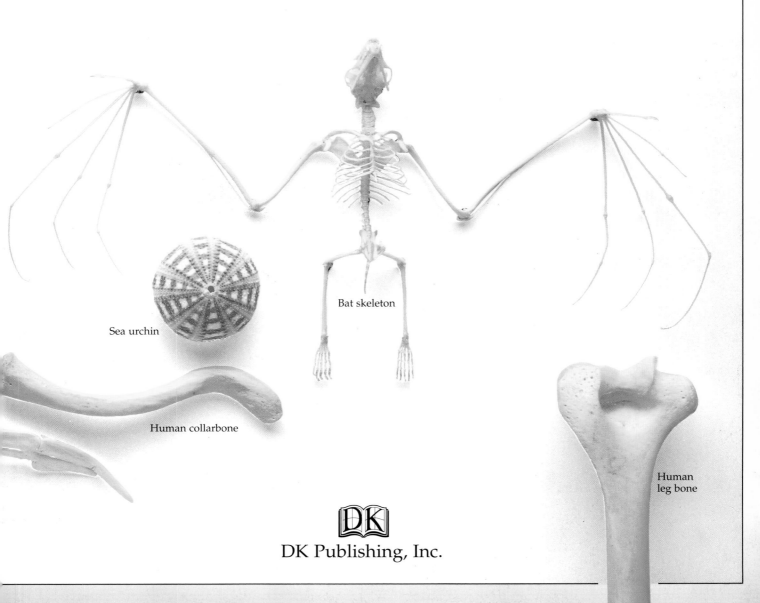

Sea urchin

Bat skeleton

Human collarbone

Human leg bone

DK Publishing, Inc.

Fox skull

Lizard skeleton

Cuttlebo

Scallop shell

DK

LONDON, NEW YORK, MELBOURNE,
MUNICH, and DELHI

Project editor Sophie Mitchell
Managing art editor Jane Owen
Assistant designer Martyn Foote
Special photography Philip Dowell
Editorial consultants
The staff of The Natural History Museum, London

REVISED EDITION
Managing editor Andrew Macintyre
Managing art editor Jane Thomas
Editor and reference compiler Mary Atkinson
Art editor Chris Fraser
Production Jenny Jacoby
Picture research Sarah Pownall
DTP designer Siu Ho

U.S. editor Elizabeth Hester
Senior editor Beth Sutinis
Art director Dirk Kaufman
U.S. production Chris Avgherinos
U.S. DTP designer Milos Orlovic

This Eyewitness ® Guide has been conceived by
Dorling Kindersley Limited and Editions Gallimard

This edition published in the United States in 2004
by DK Publishing, Inc., 375 Hudson Street, New York, New York 10014

04 05 06 07 08 10 9 8 7 6 5 4 3 2 1

Copyright © 1988, © 2004, Dorling Kindersley Limited

A catalog record for this book is
available from the Library of Congress.

ISBN 0-7566-0727-2 (HC) 0-7566-0726-4 (Library Binding)

Color reproduction by Colourscan, Singapore
Printed in China by Toppan Printing Co. (Shenzhen), Ltd.

Discover more at
www.dk.com

Human
rib

Human
forearm bone

Whelk sh

Bird-wi
skelet

Contents

Crow skull

Parrot skull

The human skeleton

A SKELETON IS MANY THINGS: symbol of danger and death, a key that opens any door, a secret kept in a closet, the outline of a novel or grand plan . . . and the 200-odd bones that hold up each human body. Our skeleton supports, moves and protects. It is both rigid and flexible. Individual bones are stiff and unyielding, forming an internal framework that supports the rest of the body and stops it collapsing into a jelly-like heap. Bones together, linked by movable joints and worked by muscles, form a system of girders, levers and pincers that can pick pick an apple from a tree or move the body forward at 20 mph (32 kph). The skeleton protects our most delicate and important organs: the skull shields the brain, and the ribs guard the heart and lungs. The human skeleton follows the basic design found in the 40,000 or so species of backboned animals. But the endless variety of animals has a correspondingly endless variety of skeletons, as this book sets out to show.

BIG HEA
In relation to body siz
the human skull hous
one of the biggest brai
in the animal world (p. 2

EARLY IMPRESSION *above*
Medical textbooks of the 18th and 19th centuries would have contained detailed illustrations such as this.

ANATOMY LECTURE *below*
A medieval lecture theater populated by human and animal skeletons.

MEDIEVAL MEDICINE
The surgeon points out details of the rib cage to a 15th-century student.

**FOO
PROCESSO**
Human teeth chop th
way through about 500
(half a ton)
food each year (p. 2

MEASURING THE SKU
The craniometer, a device f
measuring skull size - an
by deductio
brain siz

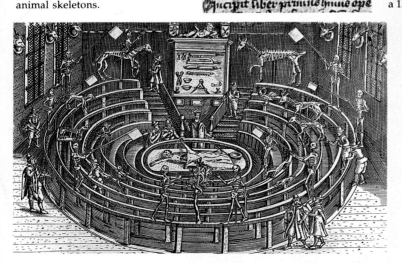

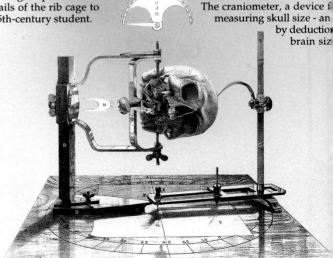

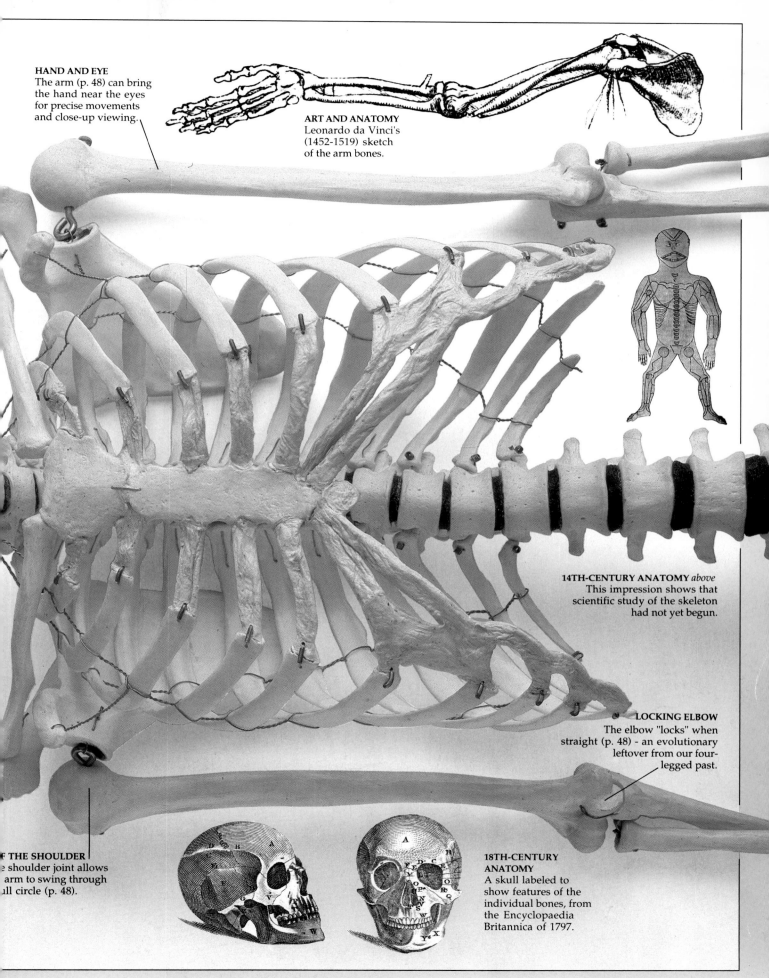

HAND AND EYE
The arm (p. 48) can bring the hand near the eyes for precise movements and close-up viewing.

ART AND ANATOMY
Leonardo da Vinci's (1452-1519) sketch of the arm bones.

14TH-CENTURY ANATOMY *above*
This impression shows that scientific study of the skeleton had not yet begun.

LOCKING ELBOW
The elbow "locks" when straight (p. 48) - an evolutionary leftover from our four-legged past.

F THE SHOULDER
e shoulder joint allows
arm to swing through
ll circle (p. 48).

18TH-CENTURY ANATOMY
A skull labeled to show features of the individual bones, from the Encyclopaedia Britannica of 1797.

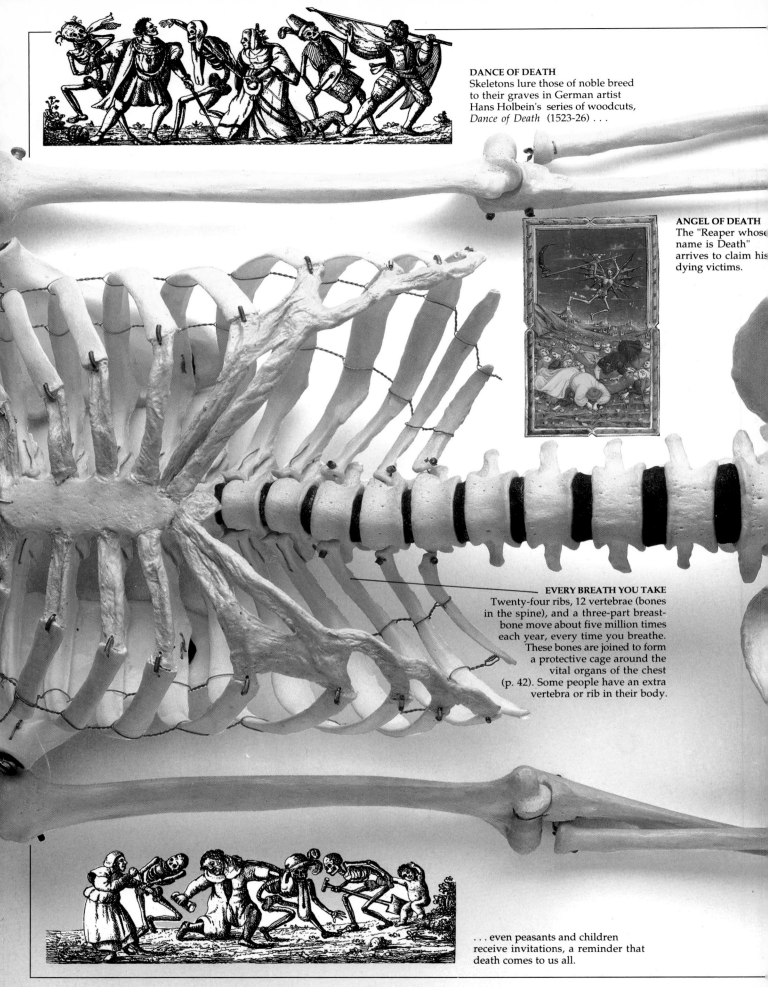

DANCE OF DEATH
Skeletons lure those of noble breed
to their graves in German artist
Hans Holbein's series of woodcuts,
Dance of Death (1523-26) . . .

ANGEL OF DEATH
The "Reaper whose
name is Death"
arrives to claim his
dying victims.

EVERY BREATH YOU TAKE
Twenty-four ribs, 12 vertebrae (bones
in the spine), and a three-part breastbone move about five million times
each year, every time you breathe.
These bones are joined to form
a protective cage around the
vital organs of the chest
(p. 42). Some people have an extra
vertebra or rib in their body.

. . . even peasants and children
receive invitations, a reminder that
death comes to us all.

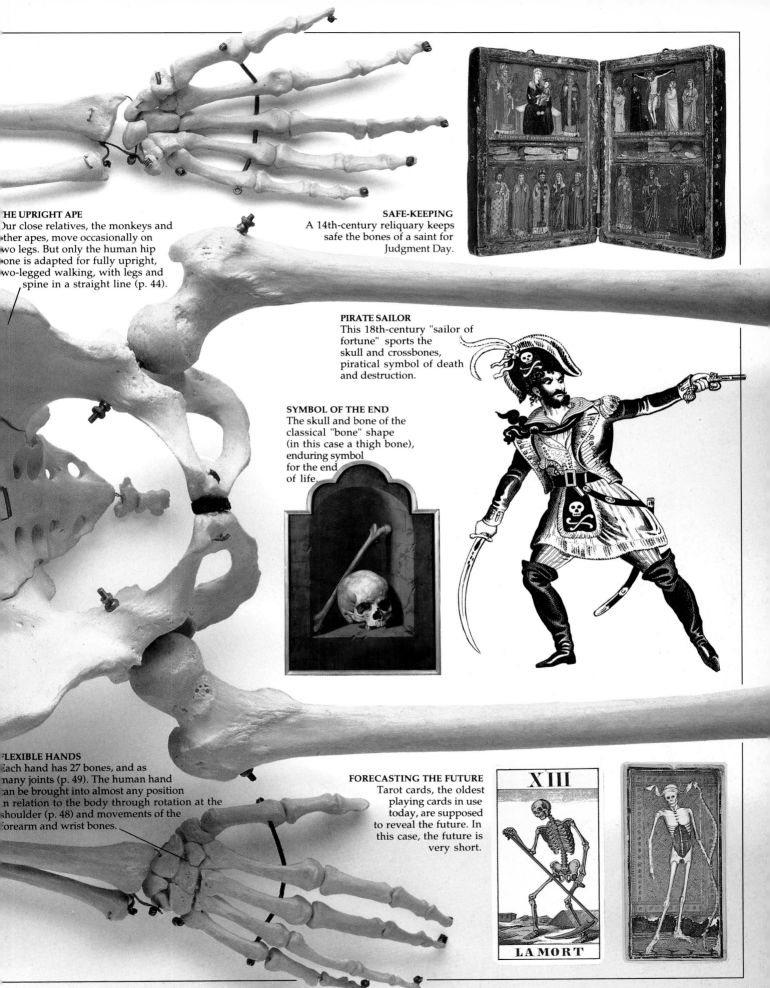

THE UPRIGHT APE
Our close relatives, the monkeys and other apes, move occasionally on two legs. But only the human hip bone is adapted for fully upright, two-legged walking, with legs and spine in a straight line (p. 44).

SAFE-KEEPING
A 14th-century reliquary keeps safe the bones of a saint for Judgment Day.

PIRATE SAILOR
This 18th-century "sailor of fortune" sports the skull and crossbones, piratical symbol of death and destruction.

SYMBOL OF THE END
The skull and bone of the classical "bone" shape (in this case a thigh bone), enduring symbol for the end of life.

FLEXIBLE HANDS
Each hand has 27 bones, and as many joints (p. 49). The human hand can be brought into almost any position in relation to the body through rotation at the shoulder (p. 48) and movements of the forearm and wrist bones.

FORECASTING THE FUTURE
Tarot cards, the oldest playing cards in use today, are supposed to reveal the future. In this case, the future is very short.

XIII

LA MORT

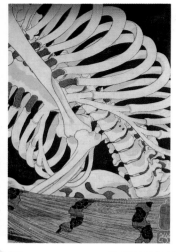

EASTERN MAGIC
Mitsukuni, a Japanese sorceress, summons up a giant skeleton to frighten her enemies in this painting by Kuniyoshi.

THE LONGEST BONES
The bones in the leg are the longest in the human body (p. 54). The leg bones are shaped to allow their lower ends - at the ankles and knees - to touch, while the tops of the thigh bones - at the hip - may be more than 1 ft (30 cm) apart.

MARKING TIME *left*
The seconds tick by for this silver skull - it is the case for a watch, made in Germany in about 1620.

Detail of distorted skull shown in the painting on the right

ARTIST'S ILLUSION
Hans Holbein's *The Ambassadors* (1533) records the opulence of Henry VIII's court;

the odd shape in the foreground is a distorted skull, seen more clearly from one side and very close. (The name Holbein can be translated as "hollow bone".)

THE LOCKING KNEE
The knee is the largest joint in the body (p. 54), carrying as it does almost half the body's weight. It forms a locking hinge that bends in one direction only.

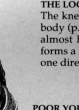

ALAS, POOR YORICK . . .
Shakespeare's Hamlet (portrayed by a French actor) ponders the skull of the Danish court jester Yorick: "That skull had a tongue in it, and could sing once . . ."

SKULL CUP
The holy lamas (priests) of Tibet use ceremonial cups like this, made from the top of a human skull, symbol of consuming the mind of another.

BATTLING BONES
The Greek mythological hero Jason
on his way to capture the Golden
Fleece in the 1963 movie *Jason and
the Argonauts*, fights off skeletal
warriors that have sprung from
dragon's teeth sown in the earth.

ANKLE KNOBS
The knobby parts of the
ankle are not anklebones
at all - they are the ends
of the shin bones (p. 54).

IGNS OF THE TIMES
n empty chalice, a
urned-out candle, a dry
uill pen, a stopped
atch, and a human skull
he end has arrived.

BEATING A RIVAL
Ceremonial drums
from Africa, probably
made from the skulls
of warriors from a
rival tribe.

UN-FLAT FEET
Your foot bones (p. 55)
are joined to form a
slight arch with natural
elasticity (spring). Place
your foot down and the
arch flattens; raise it and
the arch bounces back. This
works as a shock absorber
when walking.

**FACES ON
THE FLOOR**
This 13th-century
Italian mosaic vividly
portrays human skulls
with worms crawling
through the eye sockets.

OPTICAL ILLUSION
Portrait of life and death
in *Blossom and Decay*
(1860), in which the
heads of two young
people form
the eyes of a
human skull.

BLOSSOM AND DECAY

From bone to stone

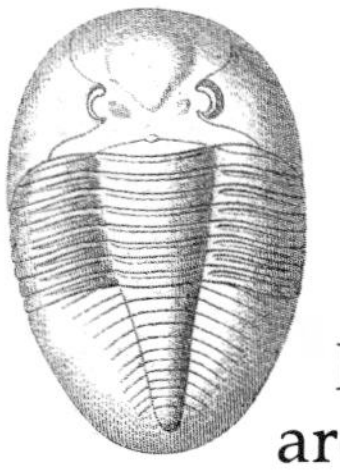

BECAUSE OF THE JOBS they do, most skeletons are very hard and durable. This makes them excellent candidates for being preserved as fossils. Normally, plant and animal remains are eaten or rot away. But occasionally the hard parts, such as shells, teeth, and bones, sink to the bed of a sea, river, or swamp. They are quickly covered by sand or mud, which over millions of years is squeezed into rock. During this time the minerals making up the skeletons are turned from bone to stone, forming fossils. Much of our knowledge of past life on Earth comes from fossil skeletons, ranging in age from the cell walls of organisms some 3,000 million years old, to the bones of our human ancestors of the last few million years.

Hoplopteryx

FOSSIL FISH *above*
This fish, known as Hoplopteryx, is an ancestor of a modern deep-water fish called the squirrel fish. Hoplopteryx is believed to be 80 million years old.

AN UNCHANGING DESIGN
The scallop (a cousin of the cockle shown on page 25) is much the same today as it was 180 million years ago, during the Jurassic period.

Scallop shell

DINOSAUR BONES
Hundreds of fossil Iguanodon bones have been found. This plant-eating dinosaur stood 15 ft (4.5 m) high. The fossil leg bone and tail vertebra shown here are 135 million years old.

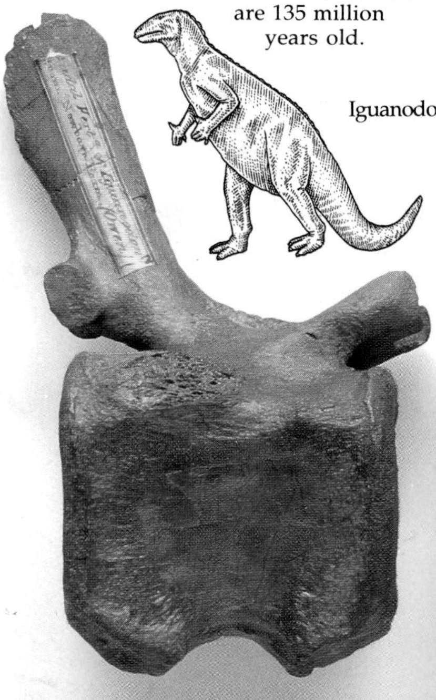

Iguanodon

Trilobite

Tiny shell-fish fossils

GRAVEYARD ON THE SEABED
Thousands of fossils of the long-extinct trilobites have been found worldwide. This type lived 420 million years ago in the Silurian period. Several other small creatures are preserved with it in the limestone.

Bed of limestone in which fossils formed

Single vertebra from the dinosaur's tail

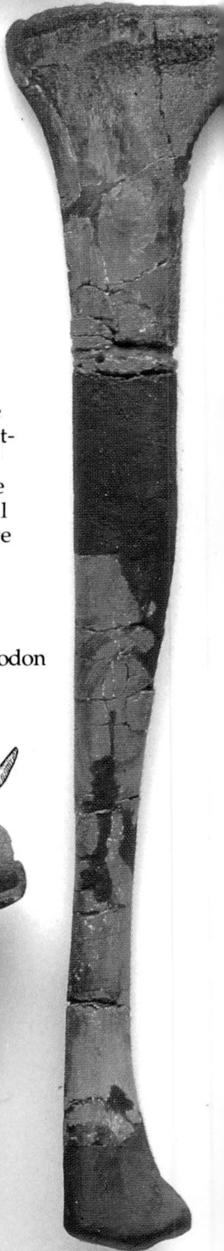

Fibula or lower leg bone

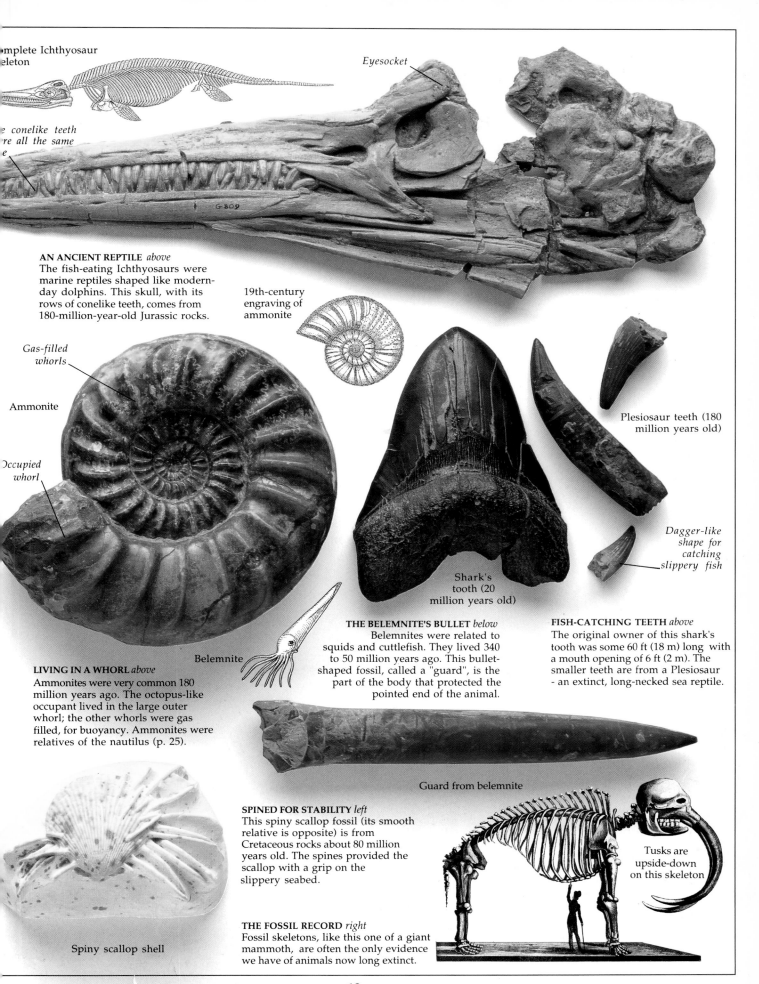

mplete Ichthyosaur
eleton

e conelike teeth
re all the same
e

Eyesocket

AN ANCIENT REPTILE *above*
The fish-eating Ichthyosaurs were
marine reptiles shaped like modern-
day dolphins. This skull, with its
rows of conelike teeth, comes from
180-million-year-old Jurassic rocks.

19th-century
engraving of
ammonite

Gas-filled
whorls

Ammonite

Occupied
whorl

Plesiosaur teeth (180
million years old)

Dagger-like
shape for
catching
slippery fish

Shark's
tooth (20
million years old)

Belemnite

LIVING IN A WHORL *above*
Ammonites were very common 180
million years ago. The octopus-like
occupant lived in the large outer
whorl; the other whorls were gas
filled, for buoyancy. Ammonites were
relatives of the nautilus (p. 25).

THE BELEMNITE'S BULLET *below*
Belemnites were related to
squids and cuttlefish. They lived 340
to 50 million years ago. This bullet-
shaped fossil, called a "guard", is the
part of the body that protected the
pointed end of the animal.

FISH-CATCHING TEETH *above*
The original owner of this shark's
tooth was some 60 ft (18 m) long with
a mouth opening of 6 ft (2 m). The
smaller teeth are from a Plesiosaur
- an extinct, long-necked sea reptile.

Guard from belemnite

SPINED FOR STABILITY *left*
This spiny scallop fossil (its smooth
relative is opposite) is from
Cretaceous rocks about 80 million
years old. The spines provided the
scallop with a grip on the
slippery seabed.

Tusks are
upside-down
on this skeleton

THE FOSSIL RECORD *right*
Fossil skeletons, like this one of a giant
mammoth, are often the only evidence
we have of animals now long extinct.

Spiny scallop shell

13

Mammals

Mammals such as dogs, cats, monkeys, and humans all have t[he] same general skeleton design. The spine is the main support for the body, flexible yet able to be held rigid. The skull houses and protects the brain and the delicate organs of sight, hearing, sme[ll] and taste. The ribs form a protective cage around the heart and lungs. Each of the four limbs is basically the same: it is joined to the spine via a flat, broad bone and has one long upper bone, two long lower bones, several smaller bones (wrist or ankle) and five digits (fingers or toes). Of course, mammals come in different shapes and sizes, adapted to their surroundings and way of life. So do their skeletons. On the next four pages are some of the many variations on the basic mammalian skeleton. Large and small, long limbs and short, five fingers or fewer, front limbs turned into wings or paddles - despite the diversity of design, the same main bones are in each creature, and they are all mammals.

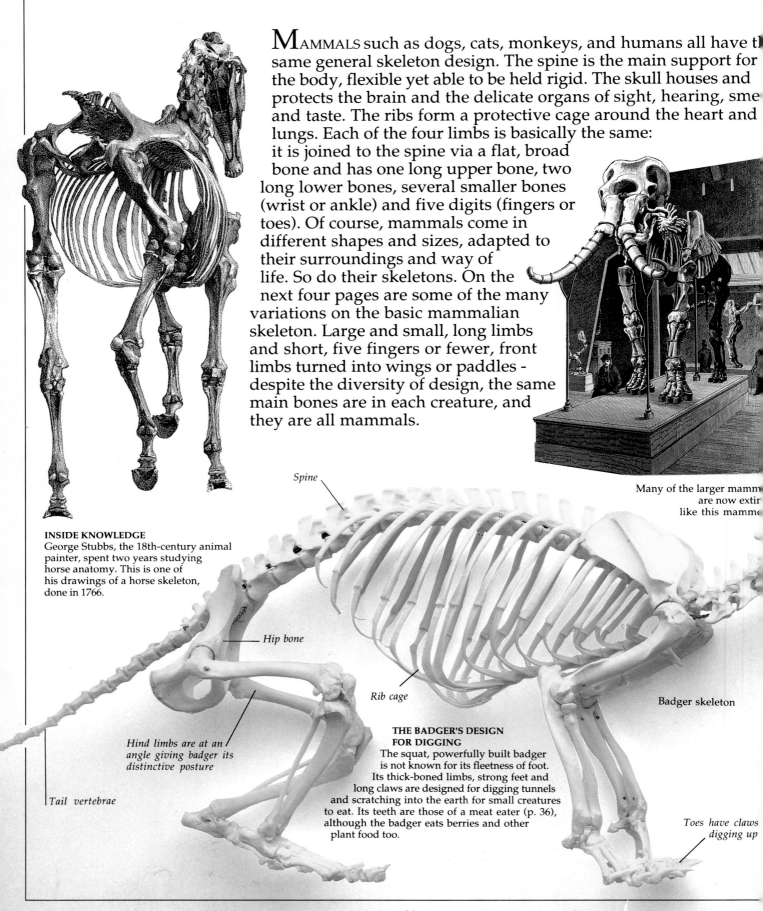

INSIDE KNOWLEDGE
George Stubbs, the 18th-century animal painter, spent two years studying horse anatomy. This is one of his drawings of a horse skeleton, done in 1766.

Many of the larger mamm[als] are now exti[nct] like this mamm[oth]

Spine

Hip bone

Rib cage

Hind limbs are at an angle giving badger its distinctive posture

Tail vertebrae

Badger skeleton

THE BADGER'S DESIGN FOR DIGGING
The squat, powerfully built badger is not known for its fleetness of foot. Its thick-boned limbs, strong feet and long claws are designed for digging tunnels and scratching into the earth for small creatures to eat. Its teeth are those of a meat eater (p. 36), although the badger eats berries and other plant food too.

Toes have claws [for] digging up

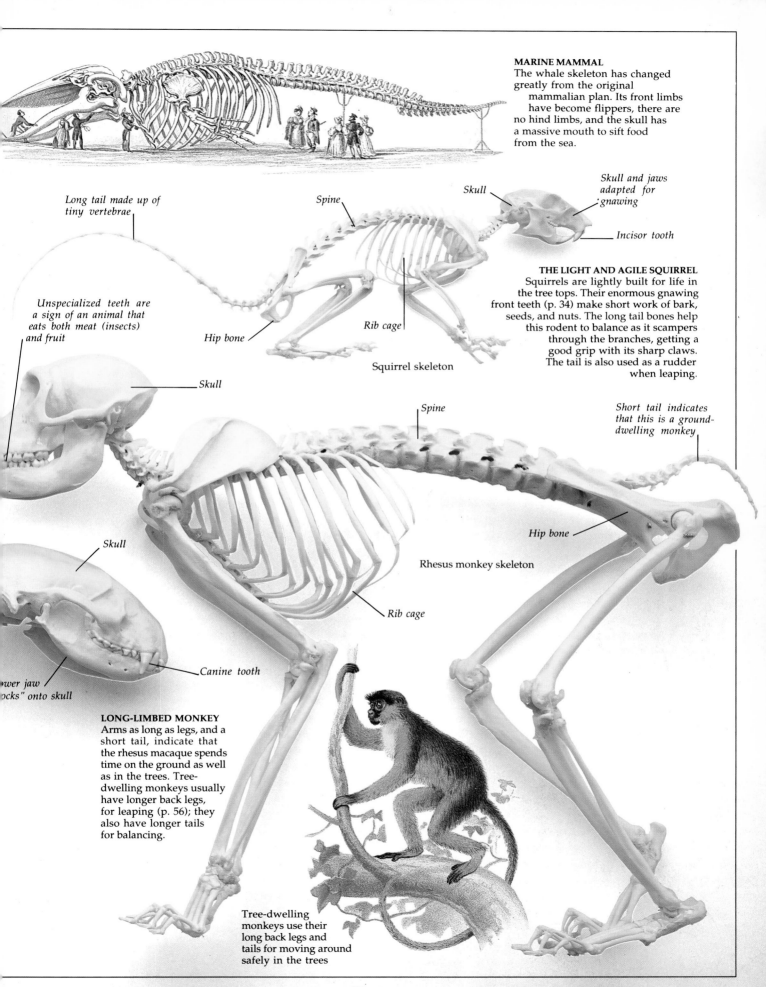

MARINE MAMMAL
The whale skeleton has changed greatly from the original mammalian plan. Its front limbs have become flippers, there are no hind limbs, and the skull has a massive mouth to sift food from the sea.

Long tail made up of tiny vertebrae

Spine

Skull

Skull and jaws adapted for gnawing

Incisor tooth

Unspecialized teeth are a sign of an animal that eats both meat (insects) and fruit

THE LIGHT AND AGILE SQUIRREL
Squirrels are lightly built for life in the tree tops. Their enormous gnawing front teeth (p. 34) make short work of bark, seeds, and nuts. The long tail bones help this rodent to balance as it scampers through the branches, getting a good grip with its sharp claws. The tail is also used as a rudder when leaping.

Skull

Hip bone

Rib cage

Squirrel skeleton

Spine

Short tail indicates that this is a ground-dwelling monkey

Skull

Hip bone

Rhesus monkey skeleton

Rib cage

Canine tooth

wer jaw
ocks" onto skull

LONG-LIMBED MONKEY
Arms as long as legs, and a short tail, indicate that the rhesus macaque spends time on the ground as well as in the trees. Tree-dwelling monkeys usually have longer back legs, for leaping (p. 56); they also have longer tails for balancing.

Tree-dwelling monkeys use their long back legs and tails for moving around safely in the trees

15

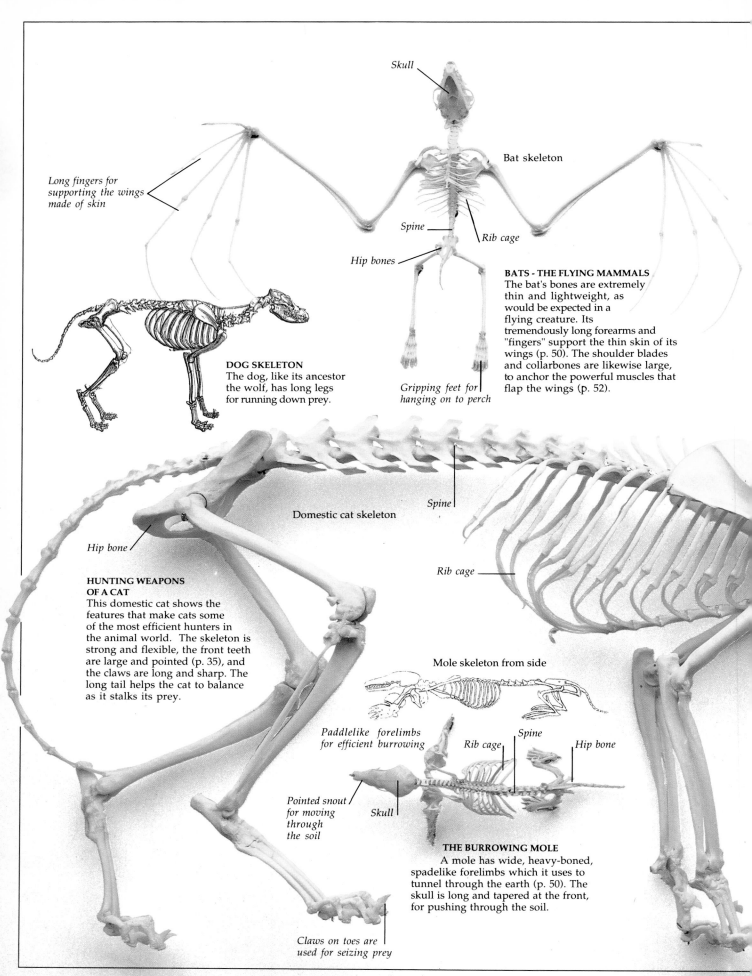

Skull

Bat skeleton

Long fingers for supporting the wings made of skin

Spine

Rib cage

Hip bones

BATS - THE FLYING MAMMALS
The bat's bones are extremely thin and lightweight, as would be expected in a flying creature. Its tremendously long forearms and "fingers" support the thin skin of its wings (p. 50). The shoulder blades and collarbones are likewise large, to anchor the powerful muscles that flap the wings (p. 52).

Gripping feet for hanging on to perch

DOG SKELETON
The dog, like its ancestor the wolf, has long legs for running down prey.

Spine

Domestic cat skeleton

Hip bone

Rib cage

HUNTING WEAPONS OF A CAT
This domestic cat shows the features that make cats some of the most efficient hunters in the animal world. The skeleton is strong and flexible, the front teeth are large and pointed (p. 35), and the claws are long and sharp. The long tail helps the cat to balance as it stalks its prey.

Mole skeleton from side

Paddlelike forelimbs for efficient burrowing

Spine

Rib cage

Hip bone

Pointed snout for moving through the soil

Skull

THE BURROWING MOLE
A mole has wide, heavy-boned, spadelike forelimbs which it uses to tunnel through the earth (p. 50). The skull is long and tapered at the front, for pushing through the soil.

Claws on toes are used for seizing prey

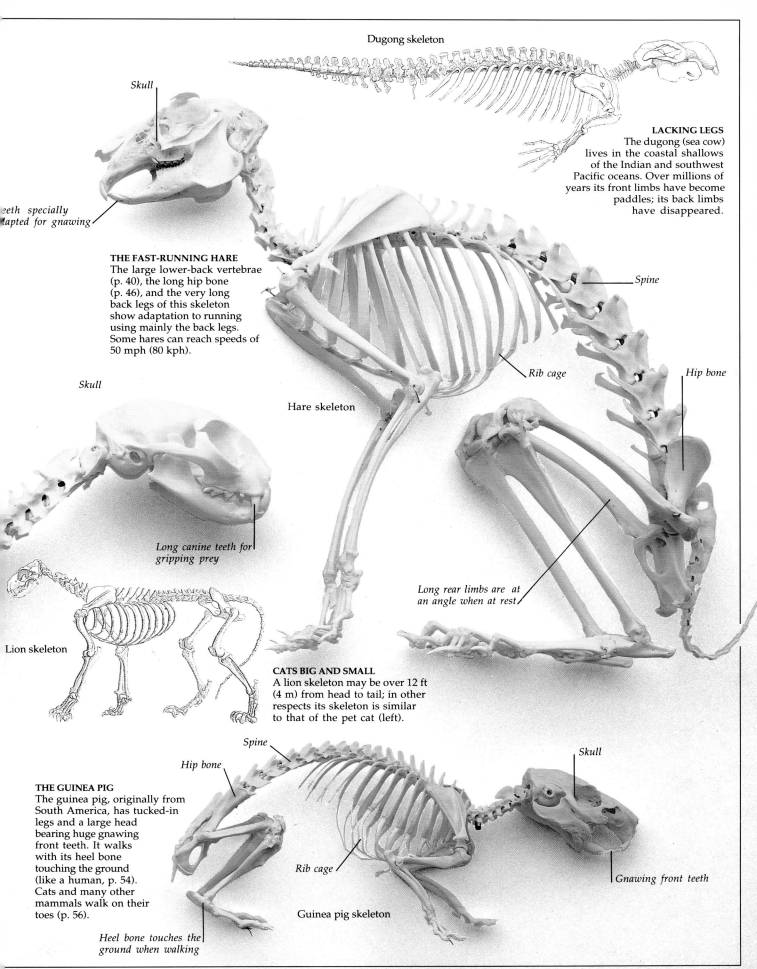

Dugong skeleton

Skull

*...eeth specially
...apted for gnawing*

THE FAST-RUNNING HARE
The large lower-back vertebrae
(p. 40), the long hip bone
(p. 46), and the very long
back legs of this skeleton
show adaptation to running
using mainly the back legs.
Some hares can reach speeds of
50 mph (80 kph).

Skull

LACKING LEGS
The dugong (sea cow)
lives in the coastal shallows
of the Indian and southwest
Pacific oceans. Over millions of
years its front limbs have become
paddles; its back limbs
have disappeared.

Spine

Hip bone

Rib cage

Hare skeleton

*Long canine teeth for
gripping prey*

*Long rear limbs are at
an angle when at rest*

Lion skeleton

CATS BIG AND SMALL
A lion skeleton may be over 12 ft
(4 m) from head to tail; in other
respects its skeleton is similar
to that of the pet cat (left).

Spine

Skull

Hip bone

THE GUINEA PIG
The guinea pig, originally from
South America, has tucked-in
legs and a large head
bearing huge gnawing
front teeth. It walks
with its heel bone
touching the ground
(like a human, p. 54).
Cats and many other
mammals walk on their
toes (p. 56).

Rib cage

Gnawing front teeth

Guinea pig skeleton

*Heel bone touches the
ground when walking*

Birds

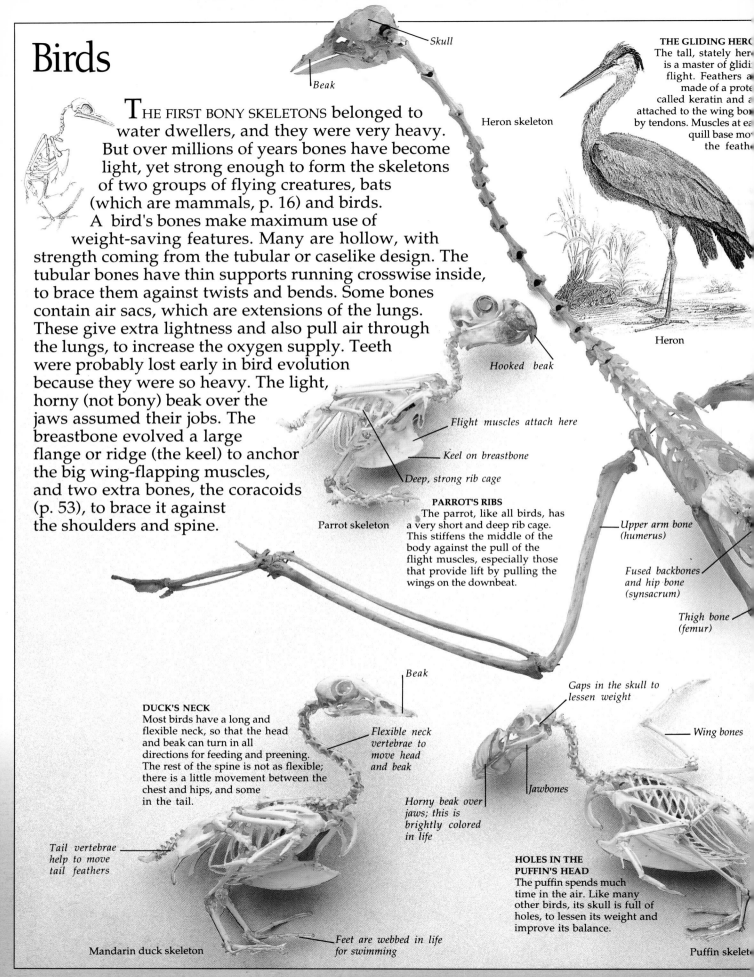

THE FIRST BONY SKELETONS belonged to water dwellers, and they were very heavy. But over millions of years bones have become light, yet strong enough to form the skeletons of two groups of flying creatures, bats (which are mammals, p. 16) and birds.

A bird's bones make maximum use of weight-saving features. Many are hollow, with strength coming from the tubular or caselike design. The tubular bones have thin supports running crosswise inside, to brace them against twists and bends. Some bones contain air sacs, which are extensions of the lungs. These give extra lightness and also pull air through the lungs, to increase the oxygen supply. Teeth were probably lost early in bird evolution because they were so heavy. The light, horny (not bony) beak over the jaws assumed their jobs. The breastbone evolved a large flange or ridge (the keel) to anchor the big wing-flapping muscles, and two extra bones, the coracoids (p. 53), to brace it against the shoulders and spine.

Skull

Beak

Heron skeleton

THE GLIDING HERO
The tall, stately her is a master of glidi flight. Feathers a made of a prote called keratin and a attached to the wing bo by tendons. Muscles at ea quill base mo the feath

Heron

Hooked beak

Flight muscles attach here

Keel on breastbone

Deep, strong rib cage

Parrot skeleton

PARROT'S RIBS
The parrot, like all birds, has a very short and deep rib cage. This stiffens the middle of the body against the pull of the flight muscles, especially those that provide lift by pulling the wings on the downbeat.

Upper arm bone (humerus)

Fused backbones and hip bone (synsacrum)

Thigh bone (femur)

Beak

Gaps in the skull to lessen weight

Wing bones

DUCK'S NECK
Most birds have a long and flexible neck, so that the head and beak can turn in all directions for feeding and preening. The rest of the spine is not as flexible; there is a little movement between the chest and hips, and some in the tail.

Flexible neck vertebrae to move head and beak

Jawbones

Horny beak over jaws; this is brightly colored in life

Tail vertebrae help to move tail feathers

HOLES IN THE PUFFIN'S HEAD
The puffin spends much time in the air. Like many other birds, its skull is full of holes, to lessen its weight and improve its balance.

Mandarin duck skeleton

Feet are webbed in life for swimming

Puffin skelet

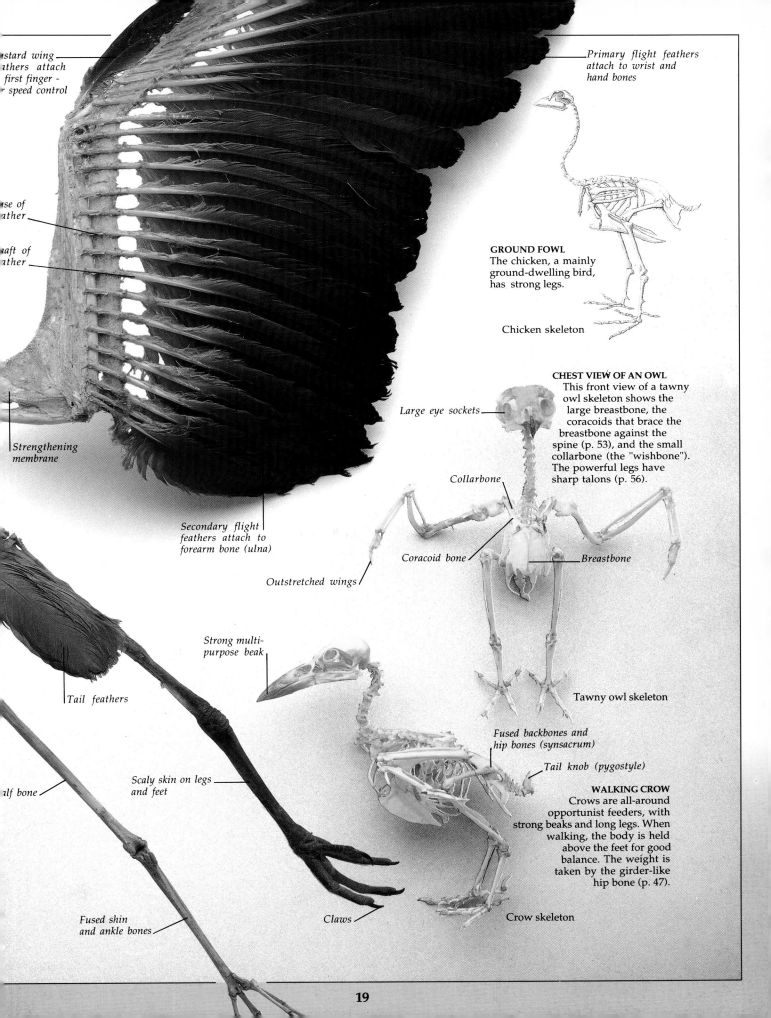

stard wing
athers attach
first finger -
speed control

se of
ather

aft of
ather

Strengthening
membrane

Primary flight feathers
attach to wrist and
hand bones

GROUND FOWL
The chicken, a mainly
ground-dwelling bird,
has strong legs.

Chicken skeleton

CHEST VIEW OF AN OWL
This front view of a tawny
owl skeleton shows the
large breastbone, the
coracoids that brace the
breastbone against the
spine (p. 53), and the small
collarbone (the "wishbone").
The powerful legs have
sharp talons (p. 56).

Large eye sockets

Collarbone

Coracoid bone

Breastbone

Secondary flight
feathers attach to
forearm bone (ulna)

Outstretched wings

Tawny owl skeleton

Tail feathers

Strong multi-
purpose beak

Fused backbones and
hip bones (synsacrum)

Tail knob (pygostyle)

WALKING CROW
Crows are all-around
opportunist feeders, with
strong beaks and long legs. When
walking, the body is held
above the feet for good
balance. The weight is
taken by the girder-like
hip bone (p. 47).

Scaly skin on legs
and feet

alf bone

Fused shin
and ankle bones

Claws

Crow skeleton

Fish, reptiles, and amphibians

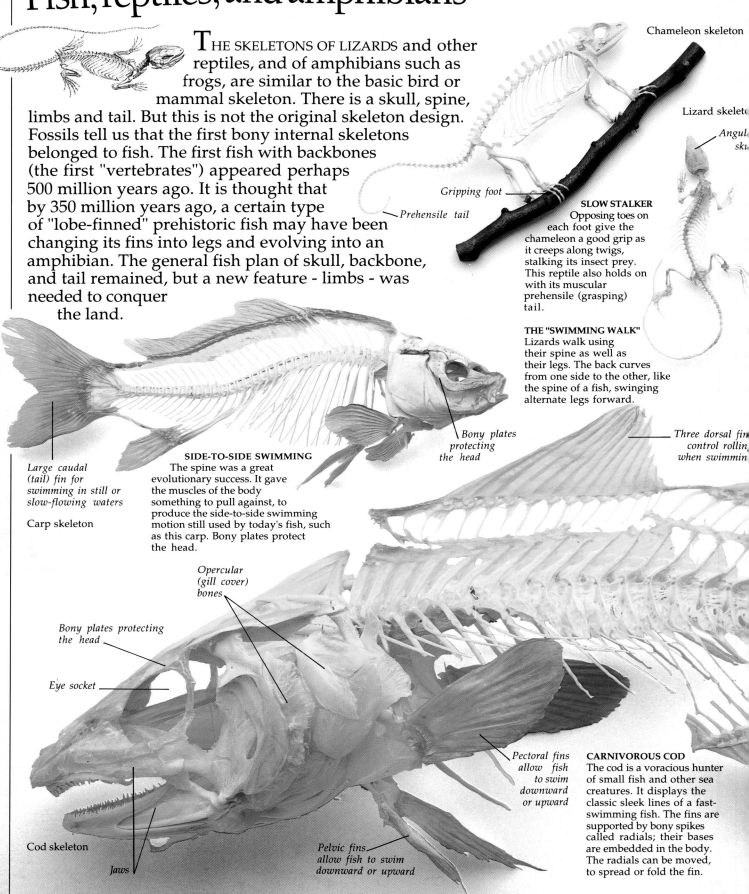

THE SKELETONS OF LIZARDS and other reptiles, and of amphibians such as frogs, are similar to the basic bird or mammal skeleton. There is a skull, spine, limbs and tail. But this is not the original skeleton design. Fossils tell us that the first bony internal skeletons belonged to fish. The first fish with backbones (the first "vertebrates") appeared perhaps 500 million years ago. It is thought that by 350 million years ago, a certain type of "lobe-finned" prehistoric fish may have been changing its fins into legs and evolving into an amphibian. The general fish plan of skull, backbone, and tail remained, but a new feature - limbs - was needed to conquer the land.

Chameleon skeleton

Lizard skeleton

*Angular
skull*

Gripping foot

Prehensile tail

SLOW STALKER
Opposing toes on each foot give the chameleon a good grip as it creeps along twigs, stalking its insect prey. This reptile also holds on with its muscular prehensile (grasping) tail.

THE "SWIMMING WALK"
Lizards walk using their spine as well as their legs. The back curves from one side to the other, like the spine of a fish, swinging alternate legs forward.

Large caudal (tail) fin for swimming in still or slow-flowing waters

Carp skeleton

SIDE-TO-SIDE SWIMMING
The spine was a great evolutionary success. It gave the muscles of the body something to pull against, to produce the side-to-side swimming motion still used by today's fish, such as this carp. Bony plates protect the head.

Bony plates protecting the head

Three dorsal fins control rolling when swimming

Opercular (gill cover) bones

Bony plates protecting the head

Eye socket

Cod skeleton

Jaws

Pelvic fins allow fish to swim downward or upward

Pectoral fins allow fish to swim downward or upward

CARNIVOROUS COD
The cod is a voracious hunter of small fish and other sea creatures. It displays the classic sleek lines of a fast-swimming fish. The fins are supported by bony spikes called radials; their bases are embedded in the body. The radials can be moved, to spread or fold the fin.

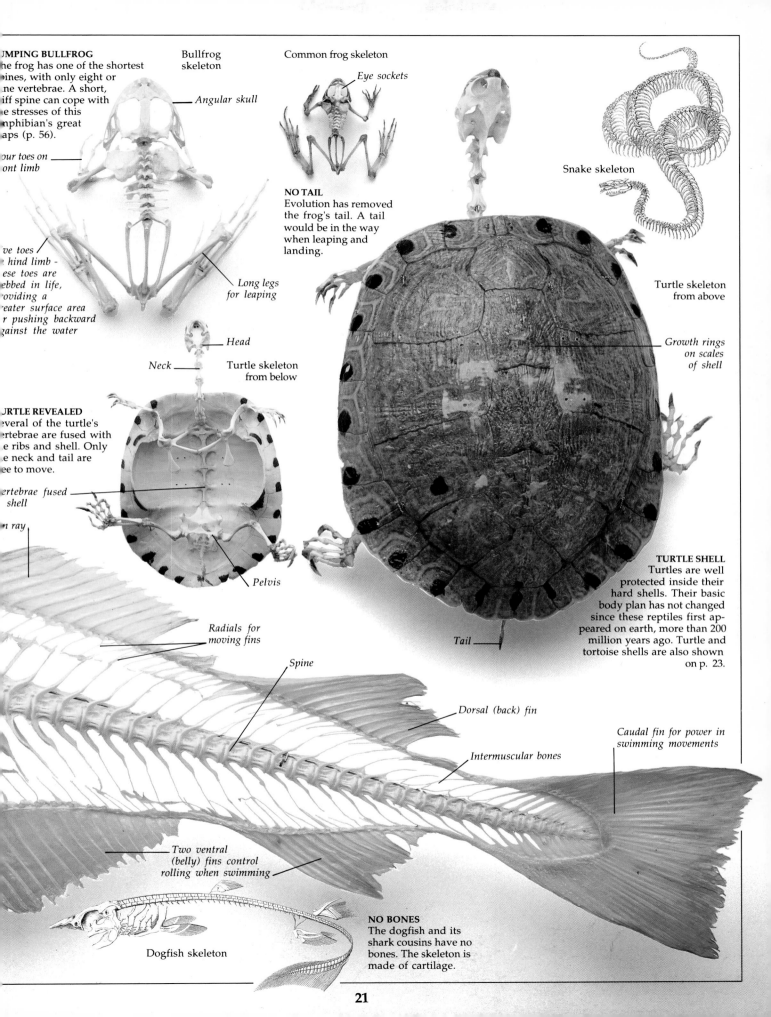

JUMPING BULLFROG
The frog has one of the shortest spines, with only eight or nine vertebrae. A short, stiff spine can cope with the stresses of this amphibian's great leaps (p. 56).

Four toes on front limb

Five toes on hind limb - these toes are webbed in life, providing a greater surface area for pushing backward against the water

Bullfrog skeleton

Angular skull

Common frog skeleton

Eye sockets

NO TAIL
Evolution has removed the frog's tail. A tail would be in the way when leaping and landing.

Long legs for leaping

Snake skeleton

Turtle skeleton from above

Growth rings on scales of shell

— Head

Neck —

Turtle skeleton from below

TURTLE REVEALED
Several of the turtle's vertebrae are fused with the ribs and shell. Only the neck and tail are free to move.

Vertebrae fused to shell

Fin ray

Pelvis

TURTLE SHELL
Turtles are well protected inside their hard shells. Their basic body plan has not changed since these reptiles first appeared on earth, more than 200 million years ago. Turtle and tortoise shells are also shown on p. 23.

Tail —

Radials for moving fins

Spine

Dorsal (back) fin

Caudal fin for power in swimming movements

Intermuscular bones

Two ventral (belly) fins control rolling when swimming

NO BONES
The dogfish and its shark cousins have no bones. The skeleton is made of cartilage.

Dogfish skeleton

Skeletons on the outside

THE VAST MAJORITY of animals do not have a bony internal skeleton. Insects, spiders, shellfish, and other invertebrates (animals with no backbone) have a hard outer casing called an exoskeleton. This exoskeleton does the same job as an internal skeleton, providing strength and support. It also forms a hard, protective shield around the soft inner organs. But it does have drawbacks. It cannot expand, so the animal must grow by molting (shedding) its old exoskeleton and making a new, larger one. Above a certain size it becomes so thick and heavy that the muscles cannot move it. This is why animals with exoskeletons tend to be small.

Magnification X40

MICROSKELETON
Diatoms float by the billions in the oceans. Like plants, these single-celled algae trap the sun's light energy to grow. They construct silica casings around themselves, presumably for protection. These "skeletons" are amazingly elaborate and beautiful in shape and variety.

WOOD-BORING BEETLE
This metallic purple and yellow beetle has a larva that bores under the bark of trees.

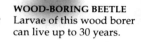

WOOD-BORING BEETLE
Larvae of this wood borer can live up to 30 years.

WOOD-BORING BEETLE
The larva of this brilliant green beetle can be a serious timber pest.

LEAF BEETLE
A brilliant green exoskeleton camouflages these beetles among leaves.

DUNG BEETLE
This beetle makes a dung-filled burrow as food for its young.

STAG BEETLE
The male cannot bite hard - his jaw muscles are too weak.

DARKLING BEETLE
Long antennae help this beetle feel its way around.

ALLOVER ARMOR
Like other insects, beetles are well protected by a tough exoskeleton made of a hard, waterproof material called chitin. The wing cases were once another pair of wings, since modified by evolution. This goliath beetle is the heaviest insect, weighing 3.5 oz (100 g).

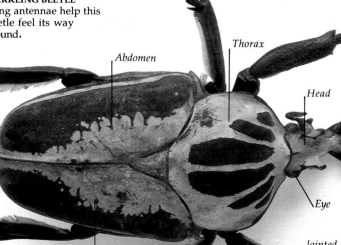

Abdomen

Thorax

Head

Eye

Jointed limb

Wing case

Goliath beetle

Leg muscles are inside tubular leg skeleton

Transparent wing

THE WINGS REVEALED
Under the hard outer wing cases lie the delicate transparent wings used for flight. The long legs have many joints.

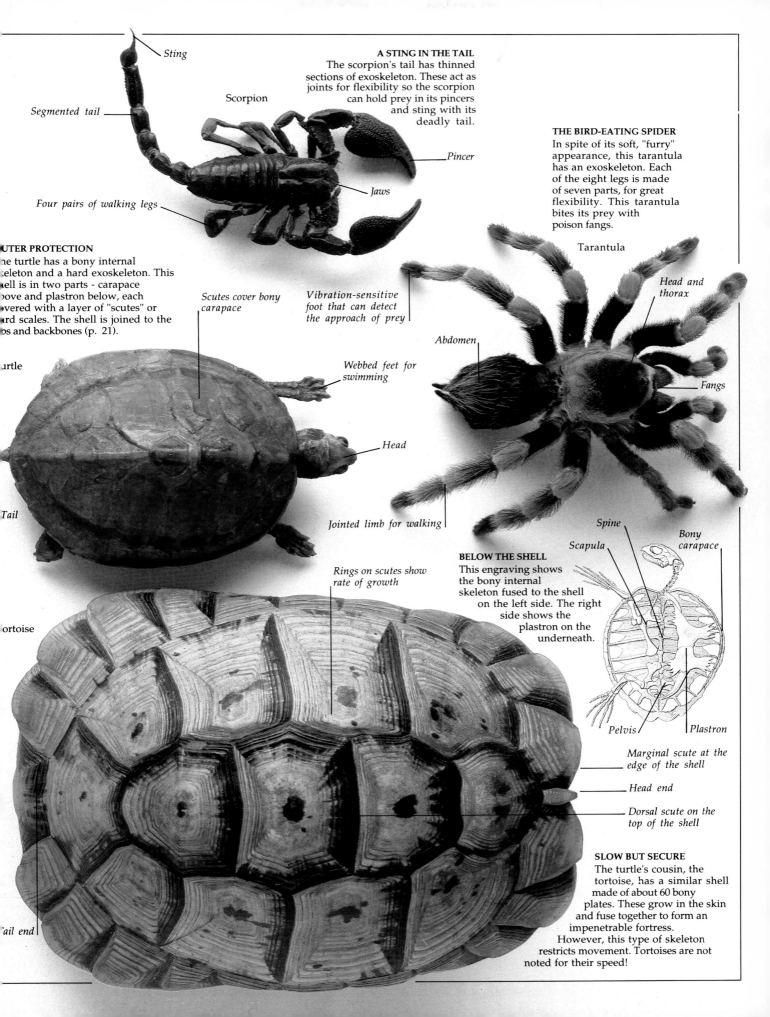

Sting

A STING IN THE TAIL
The scorpion's tail has thinned
sections of exoskeleton. These act as
joints for flexibility so the scorpion
can hold prey in its pincers
and sting with its
deadly tail.

Scorpion

Segmented tail

Pincer

Jaws

Four pairs of walking legs

THE BIRD-EATING SPIDER
In spite of its soft, "furry"
appearance, this tarantula
has an exoskeleton. Each
of the eight legs is made
of seven parts, for great
flexibility. This tarantula
bites its prey with
poison fangs.

Tarantula

UTER PROTECTION
he turtle has a bony internal
keleton and a hard exoskeleton. This
ell is in two parts - carapace
ove and plastron below, each
vered with a layer of "scutes" or
rd scales. The shell is joined to the
s and backbones (p. 21).

_Head and
thorax_

_Scutes cover bony
carapace_

_Vibration-sensitive
foot that can detect
the approach of prey_

Abdomen

_Webbed feet for
swimming_

Fangs

urtle

Head

Tail

Jointed limb for walking

_Rings on scutes show
rate of growth_

BELOW THE SHELL
This engraving shows
the bony internal
skeleton fused to the shell
on the left side. The right
side shows the
plastron on the
underneath.

Spine

Scapula

_Bony
carapace_

ortoise

Pelvis

Plastron

_Marginal scute at the
edge of the shell_

Head end

_Dorsal scute on the
top of the shell_

SLOW BUT SECURE
The turtle's cousin, the
tortoise, has a similar shell
made of about 60 bony
plates. These grow in the skin
and fuse together to form an
impenetrable fortress.
However, this type of skeleton
restricts movement. Tortoises are not
noted for their speed!

ail end

Marine exoskeletons

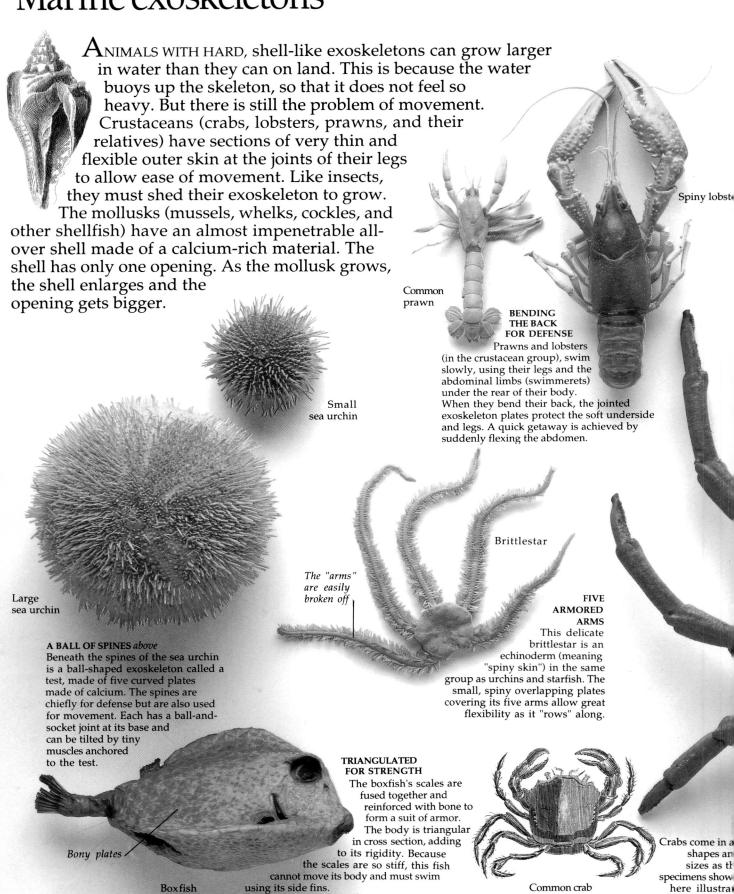

Animals with hard, shell-like exoskeletons can grow larger in water than they can on land. This is because the water buoys up the skeleton, so that it does not feel so heavy. But there is still the problem of movement. Crustaceans (crabs, lobsters, prawns, and their relatives) have sections of very thin and flexible outer skin at the joints of their legs to allow ease of movement. Like insects, they must shed their exoskeleton to grow. The mollusks (mussels, whelks, cockles, and other shellfish) have an almost impenetrable all-over shell made of a calcium-rich material. The shell has only one opening. As the mollusk grows, the shell enlarges and the opening gets bigger.

Common prawn

Spiny lobster

Small sea urchin

BENDING THE BACK FOR DEFENSE
Prawns and lobsters (in the crustacean group), swim slowly, using their legs and the abdominal limbs (swimmerets) under the rear of their body. When they bend their back, the jointed exoskeleton plates protect the soft underside and legs. A quick getaway is achieved by suddenly flexing the abdomen.

Brittlestar

The "arms" are easily broken off

Large sea urchin

A BALL OF SPINES *above*
Beneath the spines of the sea urchin is a ball-shaped exoskeleton called a test, made of five curved plates made of calcium. The spines are chiefly for defense but are also used for movement. Each has a ball-and-socket joint at its base and can be tilted by tiny muscles anchored to the test.

FIVE ARMORED ARMS
This delicate brittlestar is an echinoderm (meaning "spiny skin") in the same group as urchins and starfish. The small, spiny overlapping plates covering its five arms allow great flexibility as it "rows" along.

TRIANGULATED FOR STRENGTH
The boxfish's scales are fused together and reinforced with bone to form a suit of armor. The body is triangular in cross section, adding to its rigidity. Because the scales are so stiff, this fish cannot move its body and must swim using its side fins.

Bony plates

Boxfish

Crabs come in a shapes an sizes as th specimens show here illustra

Common crab

Seen upside down, the starfish reveals its central mouth

arfish

ARMS WITH FEET
eneath the starfish's
ms are small holes.
ny "tube feet" poke
rough them. They wave to
d fro and have suckers at the
ds. The starfish walks using
ese tube feet; its plated arms
e much less flexible.

Nautilus

Precious wentletrap

Money cowries

Masked crab

The ridges on the shell look like a face mask

SEASHORE SHELLS
Mollusks such as the nautilus and the wentletrap have a coiled shell for an outer skeleton. To grow, the animal adds another coil, or whorl. The adult cowrie's whorl wraps around the whole shell.

Entrance to shell

Claw

Eye

The exoskeleton has many joints

Prickly cockle

A COCKLE'S MUSCLES
The sand-dwelling cockle has a pair of thick, ribbed shells to protect it from the pounding surf and shore rocks. The two shells, or valves, are opened and closed by strong muscles.

Seahorse

Spiny spider crab

Prehensile tail

CHANGING SKELETONS
A crab must crawl out of its old exoskeleton when this becomes too small - right down to its last leg and antenna. Quickly the crab's soft body expands, then a fresh exoskeleton hardens over it. The molt takes several hours, during which the vulnerable creature hides in a crack or under a boulder.

Hermit crab

USING CASTOFFS
The hermit crab protects its soft body in a castoff mollusk shell.

BONY OUTER COVERING
The strange-looking seahorse is a true fish, but it swims upright. An armor of bony rings encases its body, and its fins provide movement. The prehensile tail grasps seaweed when at rest.

25

The human skull and teeth

ALTHOUGH THE HEAD is at one end of the human body, it functions as the body's center. The skull protects the brain, which is the central coordinator for receiving information from the outside world and organizing the body's reactions. The special senses of sight, hearing, smell, and taste are concentrated in the skull. In particular, the eyes and inner ears (where the delicate organs of hearing are sited) lie well protected in bony recesses. Air, containing the oxygen vital to life, passes through the skull by way of the nose and mouth. Food is crushed first by the jaws and teeth so that it can be swallowed and digested more easily. The senses of smell and taste are well positioned to check air and food for harmful odors and flavors.

THIS WON'T HURT .
Teeth are both tough and sensitive. A visit
a medieval dentist was a painful affai
but it would hopefully gi
merciful relief from long-ter
nagging toothach

BRAINCA
The delica
brain tissue
surrounded
a bony case.
intern
volume
some
pints (abo
1,500 c

A COLORED SKULL
A computer-colored x-ray shows the bones in the skull and neck. The soft tissues of the nose, which is not made of bone, also show up.

EYE HO
The e
socket,
orbit, pr
tects t
eyeba
which is
sphere abo
1 in (25 m
across. T
socket
larg
sandwiche
between t
eyeball a
the socket a
cushioning pa
of fat, nerves, an
blood vessels, an
the muscles th
move the ey

Incisor tooth

Canine tooth

Premolar tooth

Molar tooth

Roof of mouth

Nasal passages
and sinuses

Lower jaw
fits here

Hole for carotid
artery

Uppermost
vertebra
fits here

Outer
ear
canal

NERVE HO
Many nerves lead
and from the bra
through holes in t
skull. This hole, t
infra-orbit
foramen, is for ner
branches from t
upper incisor, canii
and premolar teet

**THE BASE OF
THE SKULL**
This unfamiliar underview of the skull, with the lower jaw removed, shows the delicate internal sectioning. (The individual bones of the skull are identified on pages 28-29.)

Hole for
spinal cord

TOOTH HOLES
The bone of the jaw is spongy in texture and anchors the roots of the teeth.

NOSE HO
The protruding hump of t
human nose is made of cartilag
not bone, so it is absent from t
skeleton of the sku

The teeth

An adult human has 32 teeth. In each jaw (upper and lower) there are four incisors at the front then, on each side, one canine, two premolars, and three molars. The enamel of a tooth is the hardest substance in the body.

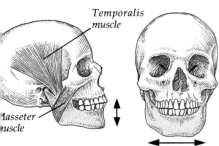

ALL-AROUND CHEWING *above*
As we eat, the lower jaw moves up and down, and also from side to side, and even from front to back, for a really thorough chewing job. The tongue (which is almost all muscle) moves the food around the mouth; the cheek muscles keep food pressed between the teeth.

Temporalis muscle

Masseter muscle

Incisor tooth for cutting and snipping

Canine tooth for piercing and tearing

Premolar tooth for crushing and chewing

Molar tooth for crushing and chewing

INSIDE A TOOTH *right*
If a tooth is sliced open, various layers can be clearly seen inside. The outer layer is enamel, a hard, protective substance. Under this is a tough layer of dentine, which surrounds the pulp. Pulp contains nerves and blood vessels.

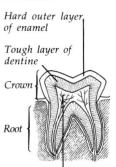

Hard outer layer of enamel

Tough layer of dentine

Crown

Root

Nerves and blood vessels of pulp

GROWING TEETH *right*
A young child has a set of 20 milk (deciduous) teeth. (Small jaws cannot hold more than that.) They fall out from the age of about six years, starting with those at the front.

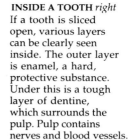

Milk tooth

Permanent tooth developing in gum

"Wraparound" x-ray of child's teeth

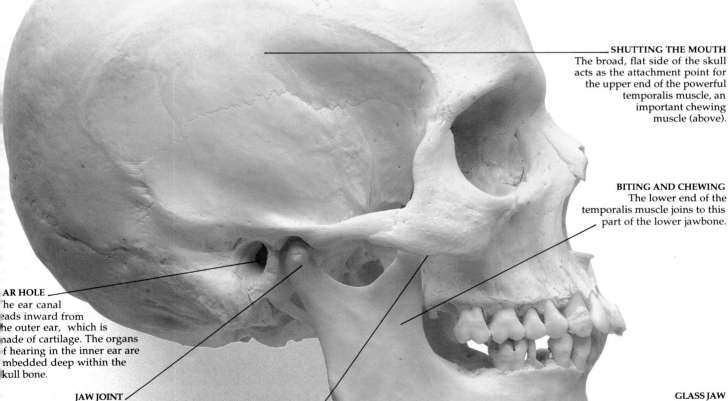

BRAIN DOME
The human forehead is more dome-shaped and bulging than that of our ape relatives. It houses the cerebral cortex - the part of the brain associated with intelligence.

SHUTTING THE MOUTH
The broad, flat side of the skull acts as the attachment point for the upper end of the powerful temporalis muscle, an important chewing muscle (above).

BITING AND CHEWING
The lower end of the temporalis muscle joins to this part of the lower jawbone.

EAR HOLE
The ear canal leads inward from the outer ear, which is made of cartilage. The organs of hearing in the inner ear are embedded deep within the skull bone.

JAW JOINT
This joint is quite mobile - you can open and close your mouth, stick out your chin and move it from side to side.

CHEEKBONE
The cheekbone is made from two bones, the zygomatic and a finger-like projection from the temporal (p. 29). It protects the lower eyeball and anchors the upper end of the masseter muscle, one of the main chewing muscles (above).

GLASS JAW
A sudden knock to the chin is transmitted up through the rigid jawbone in to the skull, shaking the brain violently inside its cushioning membranes (the meninges). This can result in unconsciousness - a knockout.

How the skull is built

THE HUMAN SKULL STARTS LIFE as an intricate curved jigsaw of nearly 30 separate pieces, sculpted in cartilage and membrane. During development these gradually turn to bone and grow together to form a solid case that protects the brain, eyes, inner ears, and other delicate sense organs. The separate bones are eventually knitted together with fibrous tissue. These joins, or "sutures", can be seen as wiggly lines on the skull. From the age of about 30 to 40 years, the sutures slowly fade and disappear. This is one way of telling the age of a skull's original owner. The cranium, or "brainbox," is made up of eight bones. There are 14 in the face, two on each side of the upper jaw, and one in each side of the lower jaw. The skull also encases the smallest bones in the body—the six tiny ossicles of the inner ears—three on each side of the skull (p.59).

A SKELETON PONDERS A SKULL
This engraving by the Belgian Vesalius (1514-64), the founding father of anatomy, is thought to have been Shakespeare's inspiration for the graveyard scene in *Hamlet*.

Two maxillae bear the top teeth and form the roof of the mouth

Inferior concha warms and moistens air as it enters the nose

The palatine bone makes up the back of the roof of the mouth

The lower back of the nasal cavity is called the vomer

The nasal bones make up the bridge of the nose

The mandible, or lower jaw, consists of two firmly joined halves

Inferior concha

Palatine bone

The fontaneles

During birth, the baby's head is squeezed as it passes along the birth canal (p. 45). Fontaneles are "soft spots" in the baby's skull, where the membrane has not yet turned to bone. They allow the skull bones to mold, slide, and even overlap, to minimize damage to the skull and brain. The largest of the six fontaneles is on the top of the skull. They disappear by one year of age.

Suture lines

Maxilla

Adult skull

Baby's skull

The pulsing of the baby's blood system can often be seen beneath the thin membrane layer of the uppermost fontanele.

The flattening face

Fossils found so far give us a broad outline of how the human skull may have evolved. Some of our probable ancestors are shown on the right. Gradually the face has become flatter, the teeth smaller, the chin less protruding, and the forehead more domed, to house the increasingly large brain.

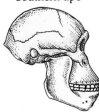

Australopithecus
"Southern ape"

3-2 million years ago

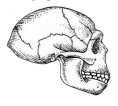

Homo erectus
"Upright man"

750,000 years ago

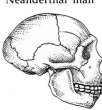

Homo sapiens neanderthalensis
"Neanderthal man"

100,000-40,000 years ago

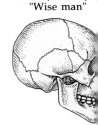

Homo sapiens sapie
"Wise man"

40,000 years ago
to today

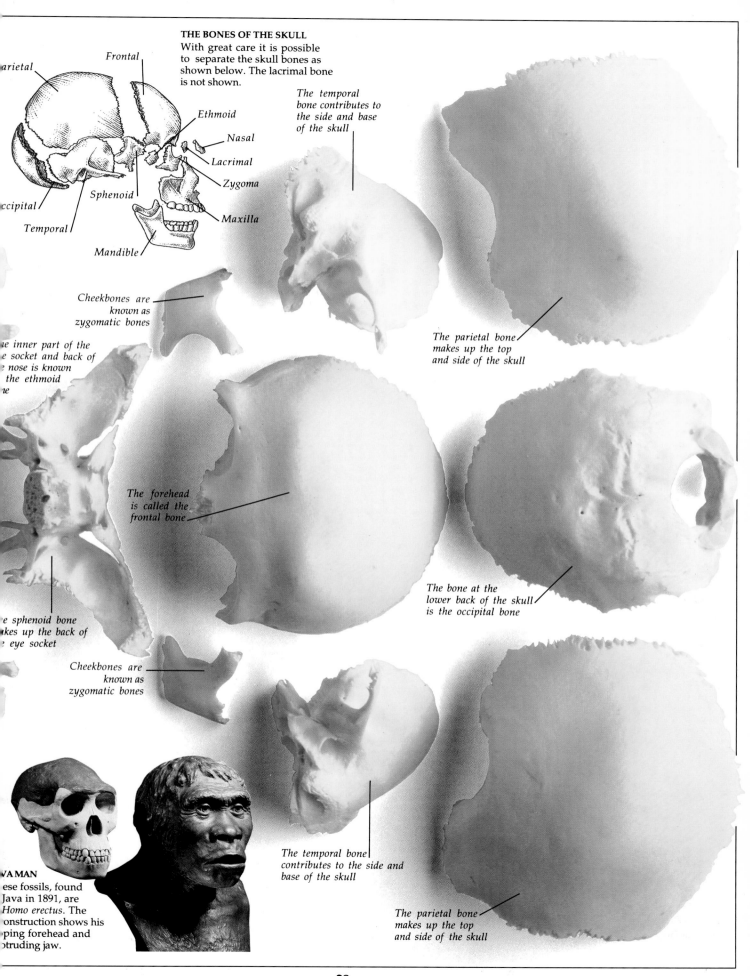

THE BONES OF THE SKULL
With great care it is possible to separate the skull bones as shown below. The lacrimal bone is not shown.

arietal

Frontal

Ethmoid

Nasal

Lacrimal

Zygoma

ccipital

Sphenoid

Maxilla

Temporal

Mandible

The temporal bone contributes to the side and base of the skull

Cheekbones are known as zygomatic bones

The parietal bone makes up the top and side of the skull

e inner part of the e socket and back of e nose is known the ethmoid e

The forehead is called the frontal bone

e sphenoid bone akes up the back of e eye socket

The bone at the lower back of the skull is the occipital bone

Cheekbones are known as zygomatic bones

The temporal bone contributes to the side and base of the skull

VA MAN
ese fossils, found Java in 1891, are *Homo erectus*. The onstruction shows his ping forehead and otruding jaw.

The parietal bone makes up the top and side of the skull

Animal skulls

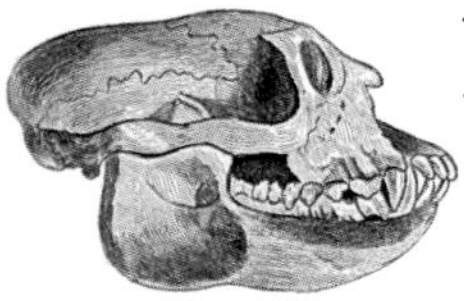

EACH SPECIES OF ANIMAL has a characteristic skull shape, molded by evolution to suit its particular way of life. Some skulls are light, with weight-saving gaps; others are thick and strong. Some are long and pointed, for probing and poking into holes; others are short and broad. All the skulls shown here have jaws: this may not seem very remarkable, but, in fact, jaws were a great step forward when they first evolved, in fish about 450 million years ago. They enabled their owners to catch large chunks of food and break it into pieces small enough to swallow. Before this, fish were jawless and restricted to sucking or sifting food from the mud.

BIRDS AND BILLS
The typical bird skull is very light, with large eye sockets and a small, rounded case at the back for the brain.

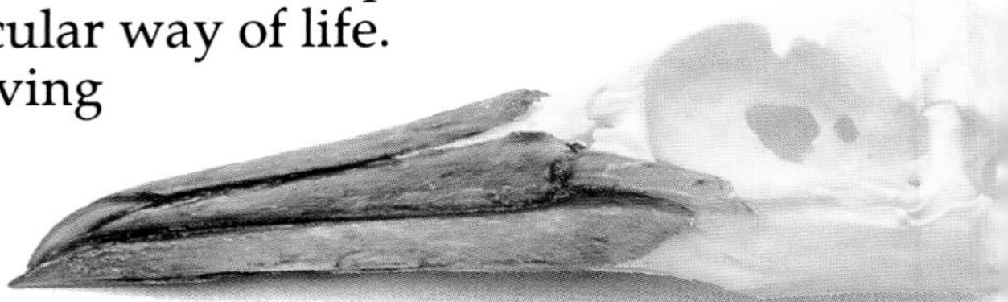

GANNET
A powerful bird with a long, streamlined bill, the gannet dives from on high for fish.

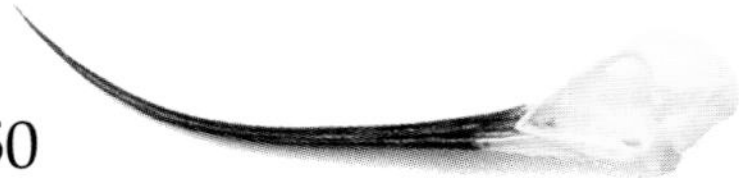

AVOCET
Upturned bill for sifting sea water.

TAWNY OWL
Wide skull to house enormous eyes.

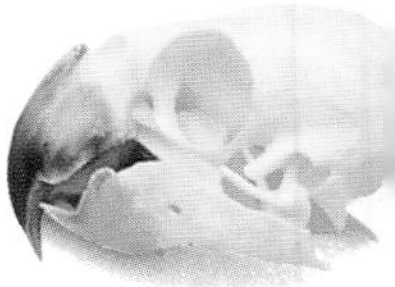

AMAZON PARROT
A massive hooked bi[ll] shows its seed-cracking power.

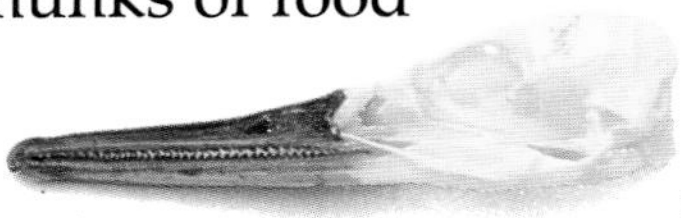

MERGANSER
This duck's notched bill grasps fish to eat.

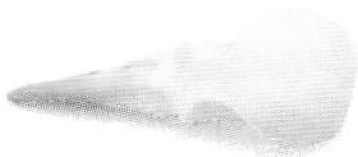

BLACKBIRD
All-purpose bill for eating insects, worms, berries, and seeds.

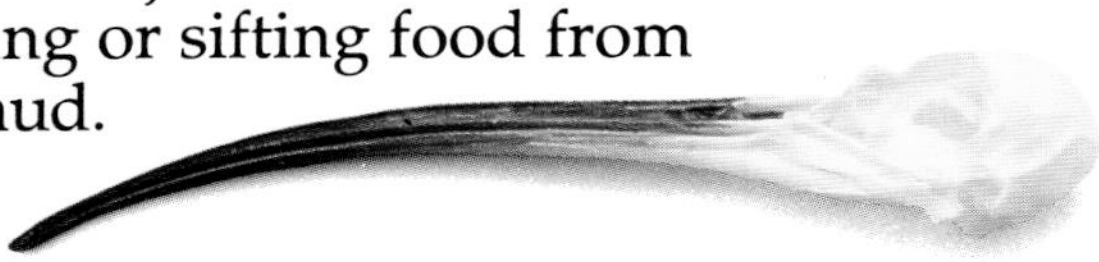

CURLEW
Long bill probes for small creatures.

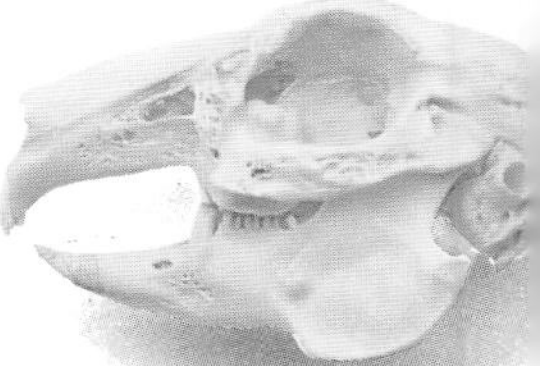

RABBIT
Its eyes are on the sid[e] of its head, keeping a[n] all-around watch for predators.

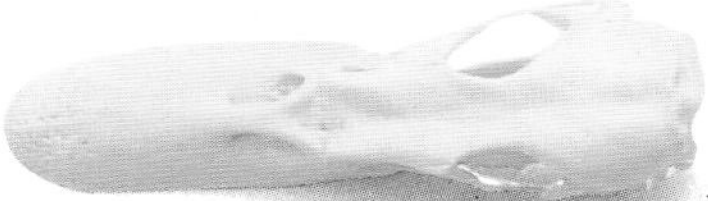

MALLARD
Wide, flattened bill "dabbles" in water for tiny bits of food.

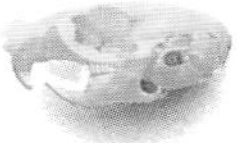

HAMSTER
Gnaws at seeds and nuts with its large front teeth.

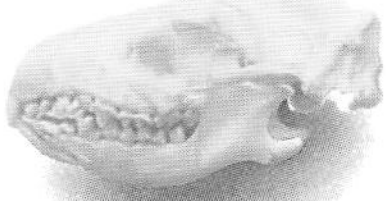

HEDGEHOG
Many, but similar, teeth indicate a diet of insects and other small animals.

THE LONG AND THE SHORT
In most kinds, or species, of animals, all individuals have a skull of much the same shape. All domestic dogs are one species, *Canis familiaris.* But over the centuries, people have selectively bred them for different features (below). Some have large, long skulls (usually working dogs) while smaller breeds tend to be more "decorative."

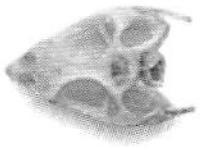

FROG
Forward-facing eyes judge distance of prey for accurate hunting.

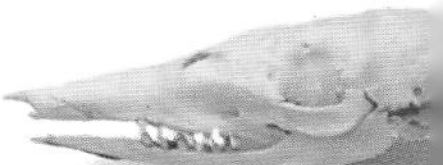

ARMADILLO
The long nose sniffs out ants and other small creatures.

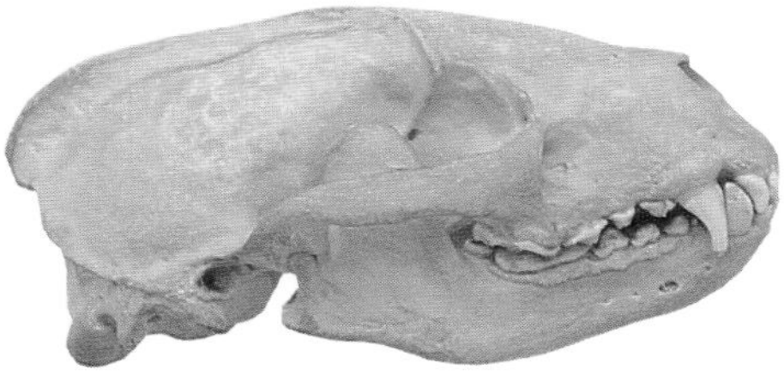

BADGER
Squat, heavy skull with long canine teeth point to a hunting way of life.

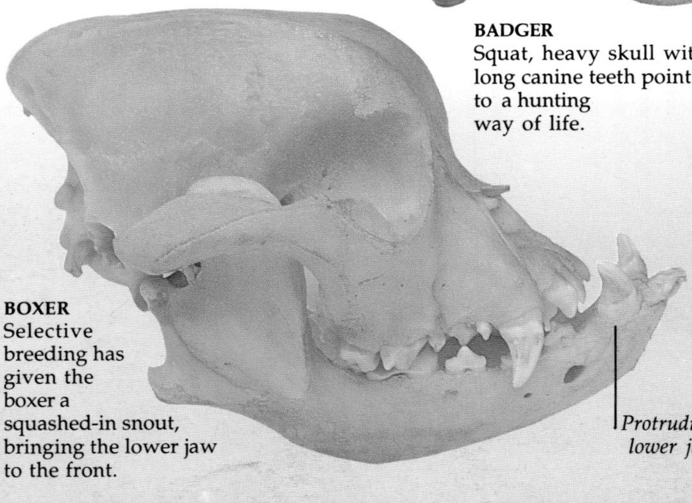

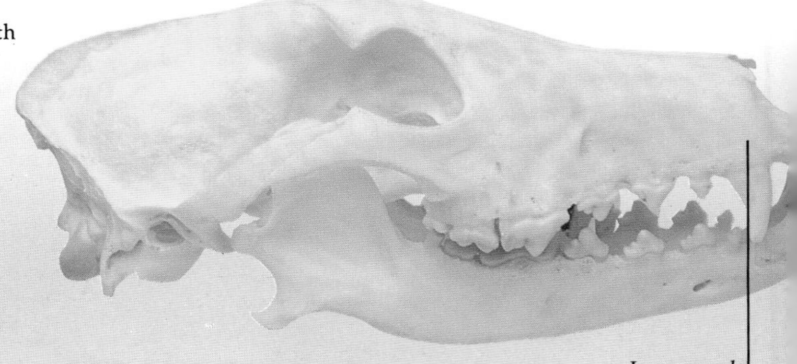

Protruding lower jaw

BOXER
Selective breeding has given the boxer a squashed-in snout, bringing the lower jaw to the front.

Long muzzle

COLLIE
This breed has the more "natural" long muzzle of the dog's ancestor, the wolf.

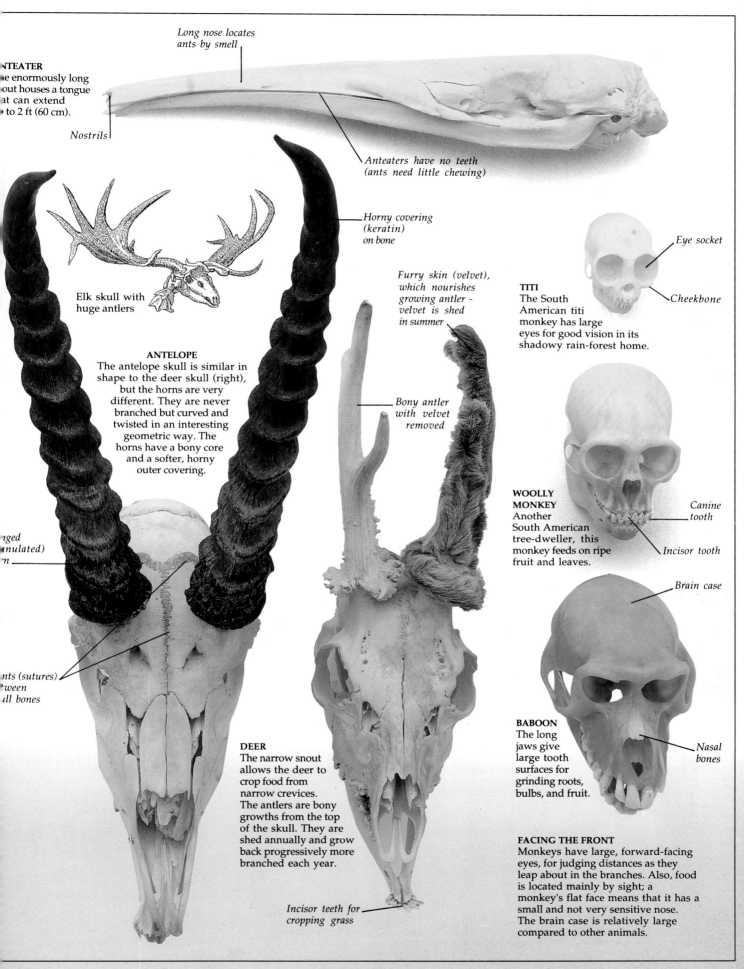

ANTEATER
The enormously long snout houses a tongue that can extend to 2 ft (60 cm).

Long nose locates ants by smell

Nostrils

Anteaters have no teeth (ants need little chewing)

Horny covering (keratin) on bone

Elk skull with huge antlers

ANTELOPE
The antelope skull is similar in shape to the deer skull (right), but the horns are very different. They are never branched but curved and twisted in an interesting geometric way. The horns have a bony core and a softer, horny outer covering.

ringed (annulated) horn

Joints (sutures) between skull bones

Furry skin (velvet), which nourishes growing antler - velvet is shed in summer

Bony antler with velvet removed

TITI
The South American titi monkey has large eyes for good vision in its shadowy rain-forest home.

Eye socket

Cheekbone

WOOLLY MONKEY
Another South American tree-dweller, this monkey feeds on ripe fruit and leaves.

Canine tooth

Incisor tooth

Brain case

DEER
The narrow snout allows the deer to crop food from narrow crevices. The antlers are bony growths from the top of the skull. They are shed annually and grow back progressively more branched each year.

Incisor teeth for cropping grass

BABOON
The long jaws give large tooth surfaces for grinding roots, bulbs, and fruit.

Nasal bones

FACING THE FRONT
Monkeys have large, forward-facing eyes, for judging distances as they leap about in the branches. Also, food is located mainly by sight; a monkey's flat face means that it has a small and not very sensitive nose. The brain case is relatively large compared to other animals.

Animal senses

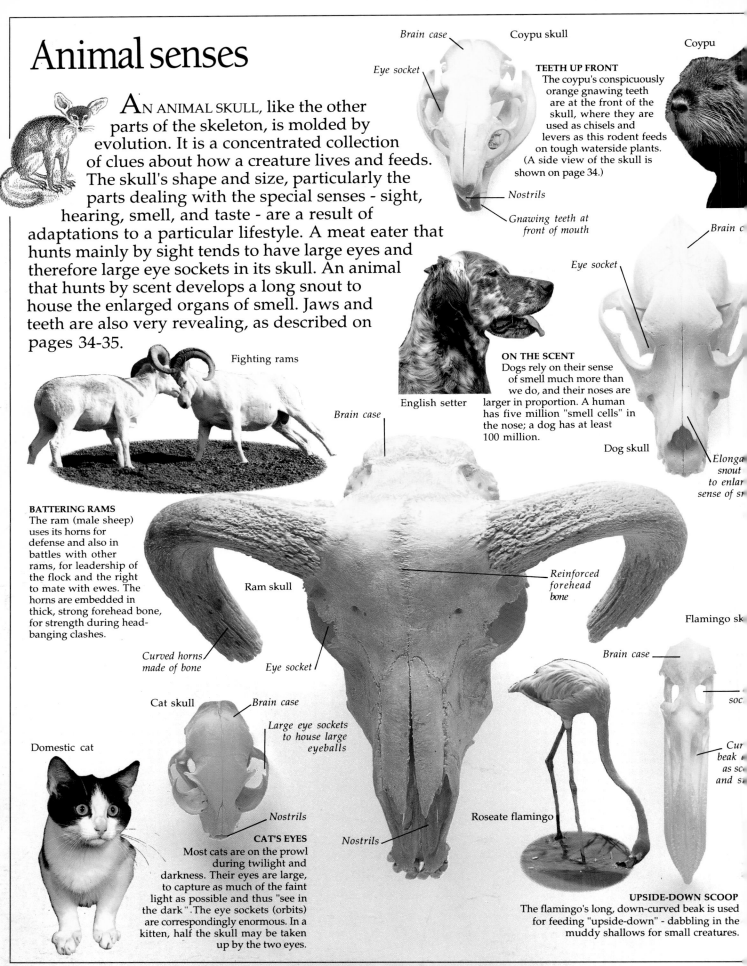

AN ANIMAL SKULL, like the other parts of the skeleton, is molded by evolution. It is a concentrated collection of clues about how a creature lives and feeds. The skull's shape and size, particularly the parts dealing with the special senses - sight, hearing, smell, and taste - are a result of adaptations to a particular lifestyle. A meat eater that hunts mainly by sight tends to have large eyes and therefore large eye sockets in its skull. An animal that hunts by scent develops a long snout to house the enlarged organs of smell. Jaws and teeth are also very revealing, as described on pages 34-35.

Brain case

Eye socket

Coypu skull

Coypu

TEETH UP FRONT
The coypu's conspicuously orange gnawing teeth are at the front of the skull, where they are used as chisels and levers as this rodent feeds on tough waterside plants. (A side view of the skull is shown on page 34.)

Nostrils

Gnawing teeth at front of mouth

Fighting rams

English setter

Brain case

Brain c

Eye socket

ON THE SCENT
Dogs rely on their sense of smell much more than we do, and their noses are larger in proportion. A human has five million "smell cells" in the nose; a dog has at least 100 million.

Dog skull

Elonga
snout
to enlar
sense of sr

BATTERING RAMS
The ram (male sheep) uses its horns for defense and also in battles with other rams, for leadership of the flock and the right to mate with ewes. The horns are embedded in thick, strong forehead bone, for strength during head-banging clashes.

Ram skull

Reinforced forehead bone

Flamingo sk

Brain case

Curved horns made of bone

Eye socket

soc

Cat skull

Brain case

Large eye sockets to house large eyeballs

Cur
beak
as sc
and s

Domestic cat

Nostrils

CAT'S EYES
Most cats are on the prowl during twilight and darkness. Their eyes are large, to capture as much of the faint light as possible and thus "see in the dark". The eye sockets (orbits) are correspondingly enormous. In a kitten, half the skull may be taken up by the two eyes.

Nostrils

Roseate flamingo

Nostrils

UPSIDE-DOWN SCOOP
The flamingo's long, down-curved beak is used for feeding "upside-down" - dabbling in the muddy shallows for small creatures.

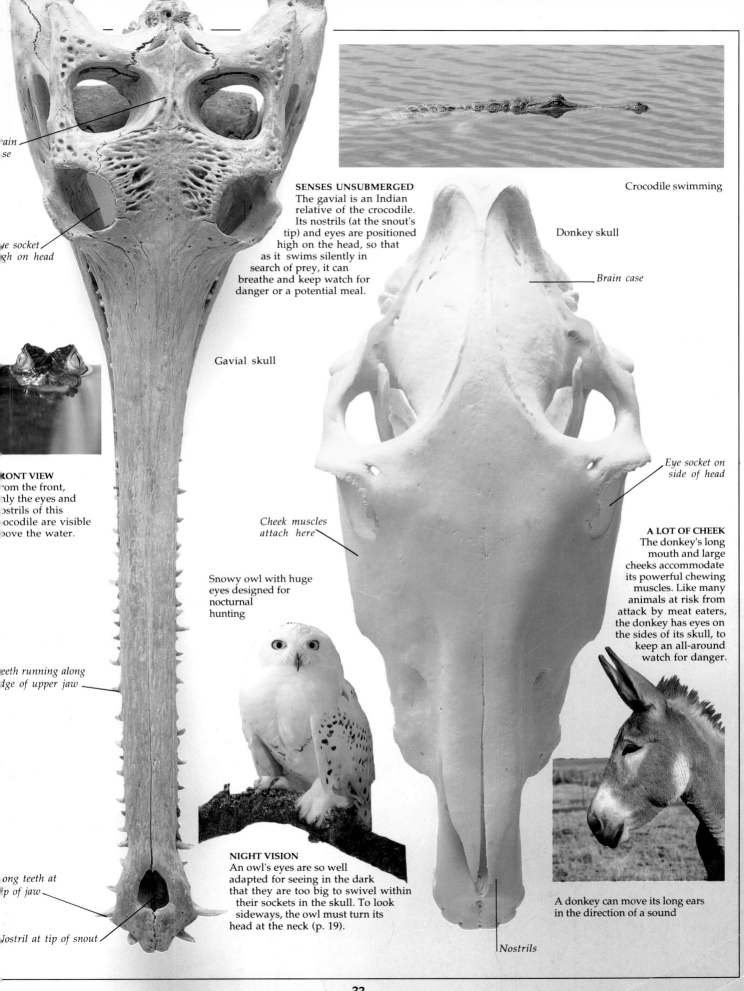

rain
se

e socket
gh on head

FRONT VIEW
From the front,
only the eyes and
nostrils of this
crocodile are visible
above the water.

teeth running along
edge of upper jaw

long teeth at
tip of jaw

Nostril at tip of snout

Gavial skull

SENSES UNSUBMERGED
The gavial is an Indian
relative of the crocodile.
Its nostrils (at the snout's
tip) and eyes are positioned
high on the head, so that
as it swims silently in
search of prey, it can
breathe and keep watch for
danger or a potential meal.

Cheek muscles
attach here

Snowy owl with huge
eyes designed for
nocturnal
hunting

NIGHT VISION
An owl's eyes are so well
adapted for seeing in the dark
that they are too big to swivel within
their sockets in the skull. To look
sideways, the owl must turn its
head at the neck (p. 19).

Crocodile swimming

Donkey skull

Brain case

Eye socket on
side of head

A LOT OF CHEEK
The donkey's long
mouth and large
cheeks accommodate
its powerful chewing
muscles. Like many
animals at risk from
attack by meat eaters,
the donkey has eyes on
the sides of its skull, to
keep an all-around
watch for danger.

A donkey can move its long ears
in the direction of a sound

Nostrils

Jaws and feeding

Mice, rats, squirrels, and coypus are roden
They are herbivores, but their front fo
teeth are large and sharp - special
adapted f
gnawir

THE SHAPE OF AN animal's jaws and teeth tells us what type of food it eats. Long, thin jaws with small teeth toward the front are good at probing and nibbling. These jaws are useful for eating small items such as berries or insects. But such a design does not have the crushing power of short, broad jaws, with large teeth near the back. This type of jaw is useful for grinding tough plant material or cracking bone and gristle. Many animals have a combination design: medium-length jaws with sharp teeth at the front for cutting and snipping, and flat teeth at the back for crushing and grinding.

Large areas to anchor jaw and neck muscles for biting and pulling

Coypu skull

Ora
enamel
incisc

Gap
seali
mo

NON-STOP GNAWING
A rodent's front teeth never stop growing, but they are worn down continually by use. The gap in the tooth row allows the lips to seal off the inside of the mouth when gnawing.

Coypu

Lower jaw moves up and down

Herbivores

Cows, horses, camels, sheep, goats, and deer are herbivores - they have a diet of plants. The lower jawbone is generally deep at the back, giving a large area to anchor the strong chewing muscle. Special jaw joints allow sideways movement of the jaws as well as up-and-down chewing.

Goat skull

Deep lower jaw for muscle attachment

Goat

Position of horny pad

Molar and premolar grinders

Gap allo
tongue
manipula
bulky fo

Lower jaw moves from side to side and back and forth

PULLING OFF A MOUTHFUL
Like many herbivores, the goat has no top front teeth. It pulls at food using its tough tongue and lips, its padded upper gums and small lower incisors (missing from this specimen). Its jaws also slide front-to-back for even better grinding.

Position of lower incisors

Omnivores

These are animals that eat both plant and animal foods - anything from small, soft berries to gristly chunks of meat. To cope with the varied diet, their jaws and teeth are usually less specialized than those of carnivores or herbivores.

Chimpanzee

Chimpanzee skull

Limited sideways movement

Lower jaw moves up and down

Temporalis muscle attaches here

Deep flange for chewing muscle

Large canines

OUR CLOSEST RELATIVE
The chimp's jaws and teeth are similar to a human's, but larger in proportion to its skull. They mainly slice and chew, since the hands gather the food. The chimp's jaw joint is more rigid than a human's, so the animal cannot chew with as large a side-to-side movement as we can. Because of this its teeth are worn into a pattern of high points and cusps, in contrast to the more rounded human teeth.

Carnivores

Animals with jaws and teeth adapted solely to meat eating are known as carnivores, and include such animals as lions, tigers, cats, and dogs. Most of them have thick, heavy jaws for their size. The jaw-closing temporalis muscle runs from the rear of the lower jaw to the flange at the back of the skull, for a powerful bite even when the mouth is open wide.

Canines seize and tear prey

Lower jaw moves up and down only

Lion

Lion skull

SKULL OF THE KING
The lion has a massive cheek ridge of bone. The huge masseter muscle runs from here to the lower jaw, for crushing power when the mouth is almost closed. The fearsome front teeth have deep roots for strength as the prey struggles.

Masseter muscle attaches here

Carnassial teeth shear past each other to cut up meat

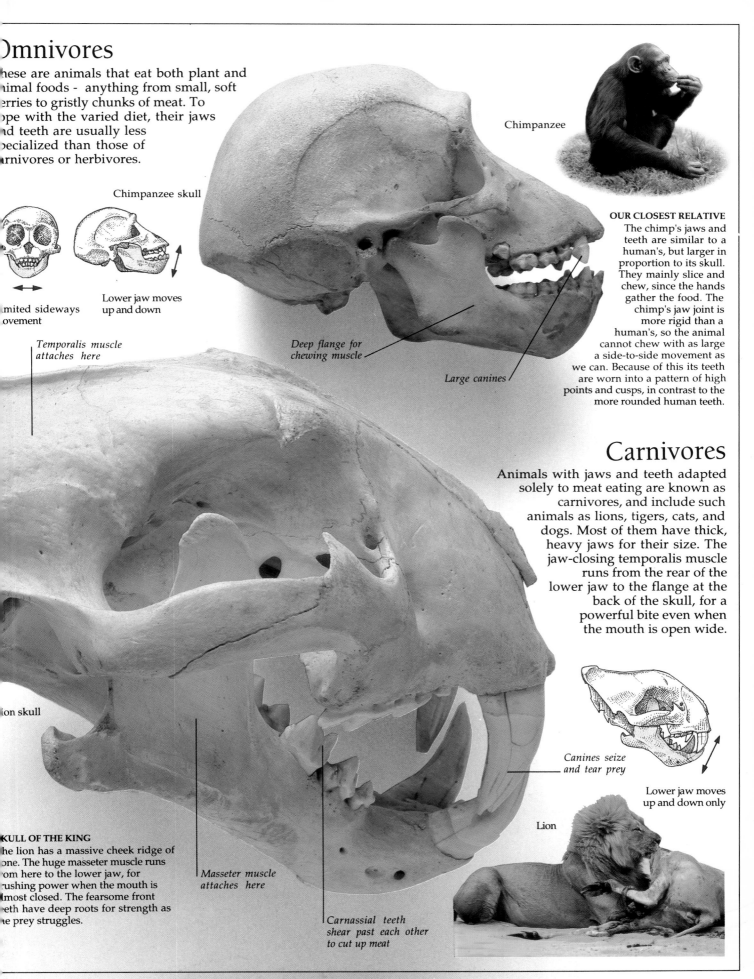

Animal teeth

BECAUSE OF THE NUMEROUS JOBS that animals' teeth are adapted to do, they vary widely in size and shape. Human teeth are relatively small and not particularly specialized we have cooking and knives and forks to help us. Animal teeth have to do many different jobs, from simple biting and slicing to chewing, crushing, and cracking, gnawing, grooming, digging, defending, and communicating. Teeth give many clues about their owner, from the type of food eaten to the age of the animal. The phrase "long in the tooth" refers to how the gums shrink in older animals and expose more of the tooth so it looks longer.

These leopards from Kenya were each made from the ivory of seven elephant tusks

The biggest teeth are elephant's tusks; the smallest, the teeth on a slug's tongue.

IVORY HUNTERS *above*
Countless elephants died for their ivory tusks. Ivory was used for white piano keys, billiard balls, and exotic carvings. The killing is now controlled, but poaching continues.

African elephant's molar tooth

MOVING MOLARS
Elephants have six molars on each side of the upper and lower jaws. These develop one by one and move forward in a conveyor-belt fashion. Only one or two teeth in each side of the jaw is in use at a time. When the last teeth have worn away, the animal can no longer eat. Ridges on the tooth improve its grinding efficiency.

Enamel ridge

Cement

Dentine between ridges

Rear root

Front root

Herbivores and carnivores

Herbivores, like horses and zebras (p. 34), must chew their food well before they swallow it, since unchewed plant material is difficult to digest chemically in the stomach and intestine. Their cheek teeth (molars) are broad and flat. Carnivores, animals that eat only meat (p. 35), have more pointed teeth for catching and slicing; less chewing is needed as meat is easier to digest.

Lower jawbone of horse

Incisors for grass cutting

Jawbone cut away to show long roots

Molars

Broad surface for chewing

Dog's teeth

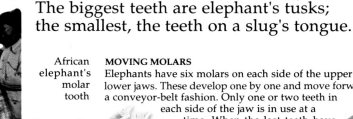

above. **LONG-CROWNED MOLARS**
The horse's incisor teeth, at the front, grip and pull off mouthfuls of grass. The huge molars and premolars pulverize the food to a pulp. They are deeply anchored in the jaws, as can be seen above in the cutaway part of the horse's lower jawbone.

TEETH FOR TEARING AND SLICING
This selection of teeth from a dog's upper jaw shows carnivorous features. Each type of tooth has a special function and so assumes its particular shape.

Bone-cracking molar

Cutting carnassial

Crushing premolar

Long stabbing canine

Small gripping incisor

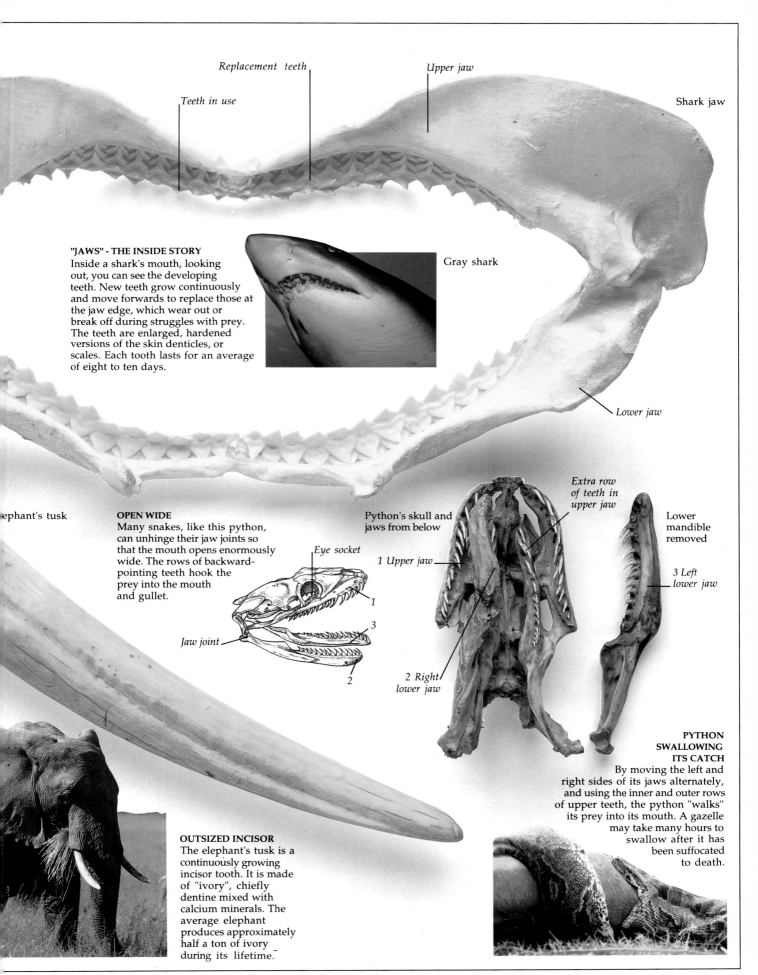

Replacement teeth

Teeth in use

Upper jaw

Shark jaw

"JAWS" - THE INSIDE STORY
Inside a shark's mouth, looking out, you can see the developing teeth. New teeth grow continuously and move forwards to replace those at the jaw edge, which wear out or break off during struggles with prey. The teeth are enlarged, hardened versions of the skin denticles, or scales. Each tooth lasts for an average of eight to ten days.

Gray shark

Lower jaw

elephant's tusk

OPEN WIDE
Many snakes, like this python, can unhinge their jaw joints so that the mouth opens enormously wide. The rows of backward-pointing teeth hook the prey into the mouth and gullet.

Eye socket

Jaw joint

1

3

2

Python's skull and jaws from below

Extra row of teeth in upper jaw

1 Upper jaw

2 Right lower jaw

Lower mandible removed

3 Left lower jaw

PYTHON SWALLOWING ITS CATCH
By moving the left and right sides of its jaws alternately, and using the inner and outer rows of upper teeth, the python "walks" its prey into its mouth. A gazelle may take many hours to swallow after it has been suffocated to death.

OUTSIZED INCISOR
The elephant's tusk is a continuously growing incisor tooth. It is made of "ivory", chiefly dentine mixed with calcium minerals. The average elephant produces approximately half a ton of ivory during its lifetime.

The human spine

THE SPINE is literally the "back bone" of the human body. It forms a vertical supporting rod for the head, arms, and legs. It allows us to stoop and squat, to turn and nod the head, and to twist the shoulders and hips. Yet it was originally designed as a horizontal girder, to take the weight of the chest and abdomen: the original prehistoric mammals almost certainly moved on all fours (p. 46). In the upright human, the spine has an S-shaped curve when seen from the side, to balance the various parts of the body over the legs and feet and reduce muscle strain when standing. The human spine works on the chain-link principle: many small movements add up. Each vertebra can only move a little in relation to its neighbors. But over the whole row this means the back can bend double. The spine shown below is "lying on its side", with the head end to the left and the "tail" on the right.

This engraving, from an anatomy book of 1685, features a back view of the human skeleton

THE CURVED SPINE *above*
From the side, the spine has a slight S-shape. This helps to bring the centers of gravity of the head, arms, chest and abdomen above the legs, so that the body as a whole is well balanced.

BELOW THE SKULL
The first two vertebrae are called the atlas and the axis. All of the upper spine contributes to head movements, but these top two vertebrae are specialized to allow the head to nod and twist.

Atlas allows nodding movements

Axis allows side to side movements

IN THE NECK
There are seven vertebrae in the neck, called the cervical vertebrae. They allow us to turn our head in roughly three-quarters of a circle without moving the shoulders. (By moving our eyes as well, we can see in a complete circle.) Muscles run from the "wings" (transverse processes and neural spine) on the sides and rear of each vertebra to the skull, shoulder blades, and lower vertebrae. This steadies the head on the neck.

Cervical vertebra from behind

IN THE CHEST
The vertebrae become larger the lower they are in the spine, since they have to carry increasing weight. There are 12 chest (or thoracic) vertebrae, one for each pair of ribs. The ribs join to shallow cups on the body of the vertebra. The upper 10 pairs of ribs also join to hollows on the transverse processes for extra stability. These two sets of joints move slightly every time you breathe.

Thoracic vertebra from behind

Shallow socket for end of rib

Body (centrum) of vertebra

Transverse process

Neural canal - hole for spinal cord

Neural arch

Cervical vertebra from top

Neural spine

Transverse process

Thoracic vertebra from top

Neural spine

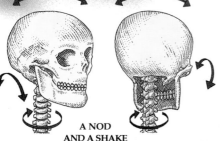

A NOD AND A SHAKE
The topmost vertebra, the atlas, allows nodding movements of the head. Side to side movements are a result of the atlas swiveling on the axis.

The protective role of the spine

The large holes in each vertebra line up to form a bony tunnel or canal. Inside this, well protected from knocks and twists, is the delicate spinal cord. Nerves enter and leave the cord through gaps between neighboring vertebrae. Occasionally, a disc of cartilage between two vertebrae is squashed and presses on the nerve, causing the pain of a "slipped disc."

Spinal cord

Neural canal

Body of vertebra

Nerves to and from spinal cord

The delicate spinal cord runs through the neural canal of each vertebra

Brain

Nerves to upper body

Spinal cord

Nerves to lower body

A CONTINUOUS CANAL
The bones of the spine lie on top of each other to provide a continuous canal for the spinal cord. This cord emerges from the brain through a hole in the skull (p. 26), and the many nerves branch out from the canal through the gaps between neighboring vertebrae.

Spine from front showing continuous column of vertebrae

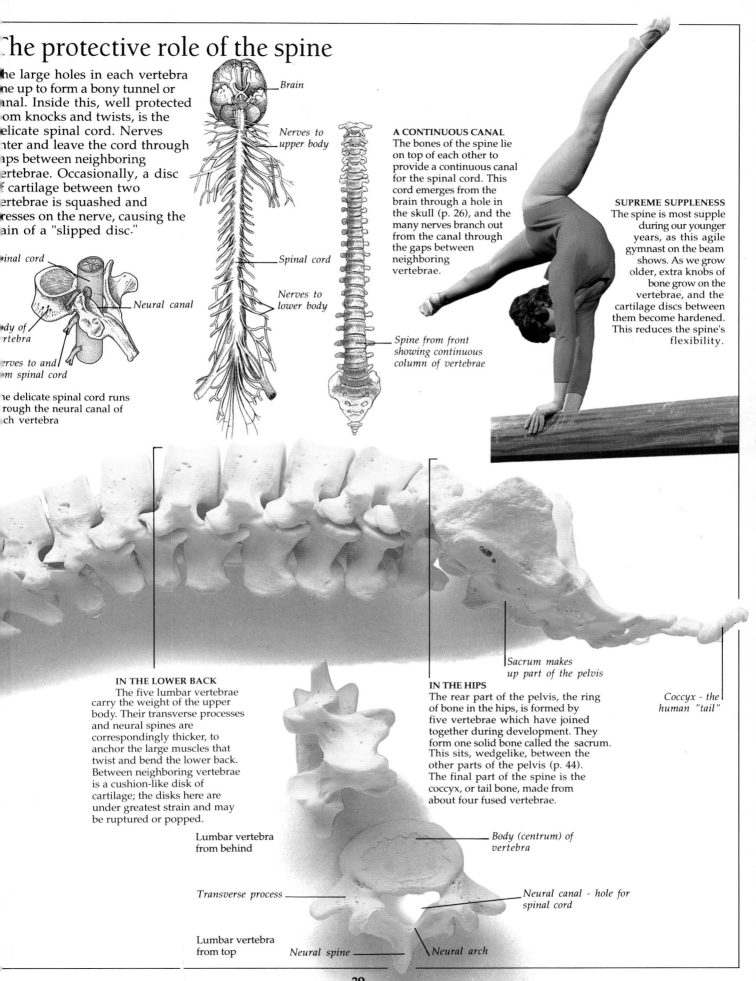

SUPREME SUPPLENESS
The spine is most supple during our younger years, as this agile gymnast on the beam shows. As we grow older, extra knobs of bone grow on the vertebrae, and the cartilage discs between them become hardened. This reduces the spine's flexibility.

Sacrum makes up part of the pelvis

Coccyx - the human "tail"

IN THE LOWER BACK
The five lumbar vertebrae carry the weight of the upper body. Their transverse processes and neural spines are correspondingly thicker, to anchor the large muscles that twist and bend the lower back. Between neighboring vertebrae is a cushion-like disk of cartilage; the disks here are under greatest strain and may be ruptured or popped.

IN THE HIPS
The rear part of the pelvis, the ring of bone in the hips, is formed by five vertebrae which have joined together during development. They form one solid bone called the sacrum. This sits, wedgelike, between the other parts of the pelvis (p. 44). The final part of the spine is the coccyx, or tail bone, made from about four fused vertebrae.

Lumbar vertebra from behind

Body (centrum) of vertebra

Transverse process

Neural canal - hole for spinal cord

Lumbar vertebra from top

Neural spine

Neural arch

Animal backbones

EVERY FISH, REPTILE, amphibian, bird, and mammal has a row of bones in its back, usually called the spine or spinal column. This is the feature that groups them together as vertebrates (animals with backbones or vertebrae), distinguishing them from invertebrates such as insects and worms (p. 22). The basic spine design is a row of small bones, linked together into a flexible column, with the skull at one end and a tail (usually) at the other. However, the number of individual vertebrae varies from as few as nine in a frog to more than 400 in some snakes!

A GRIPPING TAIL
The end of the lemur's spine - its tail - is prehensile and serves as a fifth limb, to grip branches while climbing. This also leaves both hands free when feeding.

Ring-tailed lemurs

Nose to tail length - 35 in (89 cm)

First two vertebrae allow head to twist and nod

HEAD TO TAIL
A fox has about 50 vertebrae; about half of these are in its "brush" or tail. Those in the hip region have large flanges (ridges) for the muscles and ligaments that secure the pelvis.

Red fox

Region of stomach

SLITHERING ALONG
In a snake each vertebra, with its pair of ribs, is virtually identical to all the others. A snake's skeleton is all backbone as it has no arms, legs, shoulder blades, or pelvis. Large snakes, such as this python, use their belly scales to move. The scales, attached to the ribs, are pushed backwards in groups; their rear edges are tilted down to grip the ground.

Shoulder blades linked here

Python skeleton

Reticulated python

Region of heart

Skull

Lower jaw

AGILE REPTILES
Lack of limbs does not seem to restrict snakes, such as this reticulated python. They can move very fast, climb, swim, and burrow.

Region of intestine

Rib

ark spinal column

und discs
cartilage

Gray shark

Neural spine anchors
muscles that force tail
upward, moving
whale forward

Forward-pointing
transverse processes
fit into grooves of
vertebra in front

SHARK SPINE
A shark's "backbones" are not bone at all
(and neither is the rest of the
skeleton). They are made mainly
of cartilage (gristle). The
central part of each one,
the centrum, as shown
here, is hardened
with minerals such
as calcium.

Strengthening "spokes"
of hard minerals

ps attach to sacrum
sed vertebrae)

x spinal
umn

Neural
spine

Neural
spine

Centrum

Ferret vertebra

Individual vertebrae

Take a spine apart and the
general shape of each vertebra
becomes clear. The rounded lump
of bone, the centrum, butts up against
its neighbors front and back. Above
this is a hole, the neural canal,
through which runs the well-
protected spinal nerve cord. The
"wings" of bone (transverse processes)
anchor muscles that move the back
and, in a four-legged creature,
support the underslung
weight of the body.

Hole for
spinal cord
is called
the neural canal

Neural arch

Neural canal

UNNER AND SWIMMER
ae dolphin's vertebra has
atively large bony wings for
choring the back-bending muscles,
mpared with the ferret's tiny
uivalents. This is because a dolphin
vims entirely by wavelike motions
its spine, while the ferret, although
raceful mover, relies more on
leg muscles.

Transverse
process

Centrum

Dolphin vertebra

Baleen whale
vertebra

Transverse process

THE LARGEST MAMMAL
This rear view of a whale vertebra
shows the system of pegs and grooves
that keep the spine from twisting too
much. The forward-pointing transverse
processes fit into grooves in the vertebra
in front; similar transverse processes from
the vertebra behind fit into the grooves
on this vertebra.

The rib cage

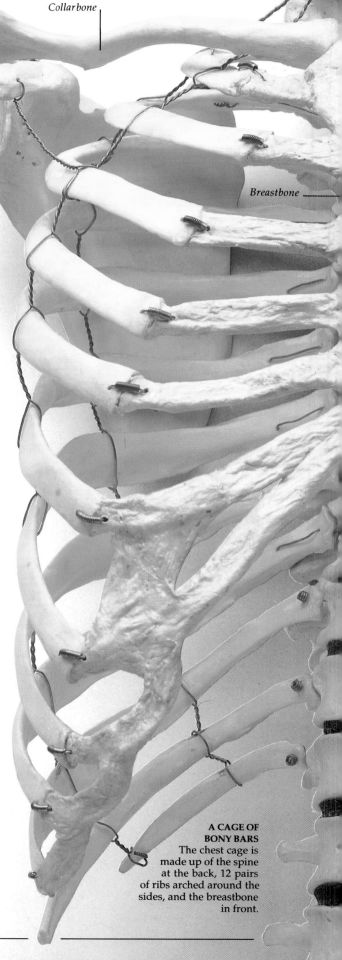

Collarbone

Breastbone

PROBLEM: the lungs need to inflate and deflate, becoming larger and smaller as they breathe; yet they also need protection against being knocked or crushed. A solid case of protective bone, like the skull around the brain, would be too rigid. Answer: a flexible cage with movable bars - the ribs. Closely spaced, with tough ligaments and muscles between them, the ribs give good protection to the delicate lungs. In addition, each rib is thin and flexible, so that it can absorb knocks without cracking and puncturing the vital airtight seal around the lungs. The ribs move at the points where they join the spine and breastbone. When breathing in, muscles lift the ribs upwards and swing them outward, increasing the volume of the chest and sucking air into the lungs.

Inside the chest

The ribs protect the lungs and also the other organs in the chest, such as the heart and main blood vessels. And they guard the stomach, liver, and other parts of the upper abdomen. These organs nestle under the diaphragm, a dome-shaped muscle that forms the base of the chest, so they are above the level of the bottom ribs.

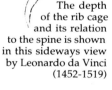

The depth of the rib cage and its relation to the spine is shown in this sideways view by Leonardo da Vinci (1452-1519)

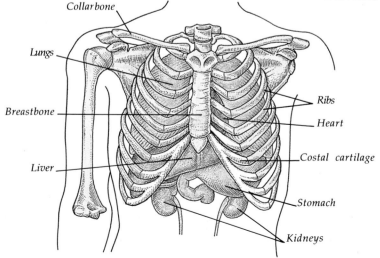

Collarbone

Lungs

Breastbone

Liver

Ribs

Heart

Costal cartilage

Stomach

Kidneys

A CAGE OF BONY BARS
The chest cage is made up of the spine at the back, 12 pairs of ribs arched around the sides, and the breastbone in front.

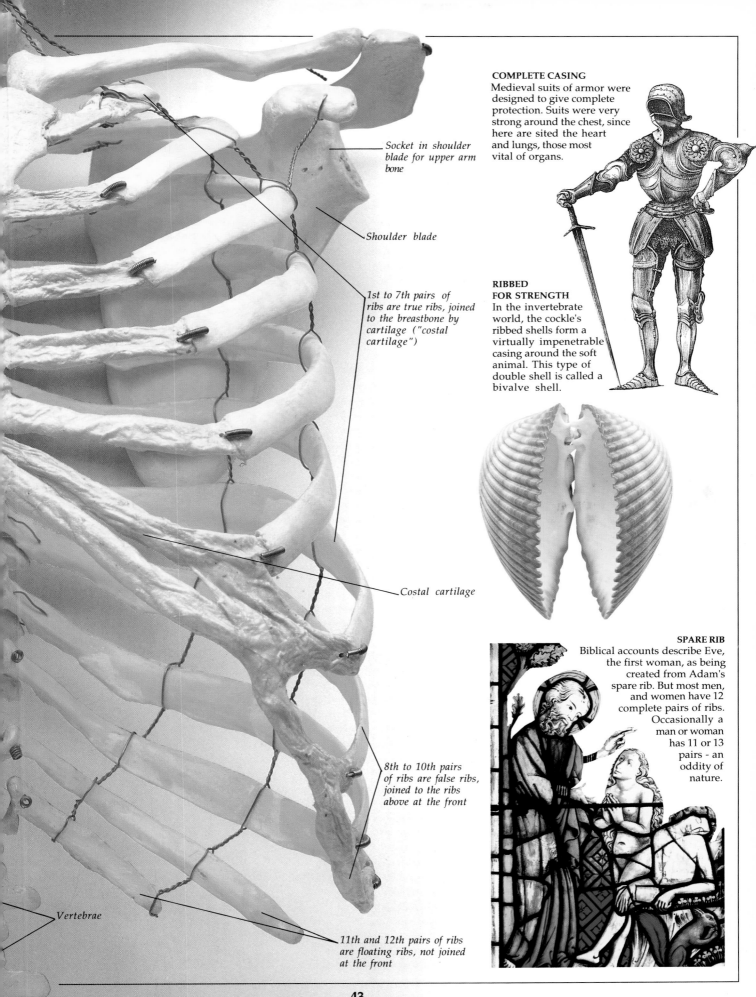

Socket in shoulder
blade for upper arm
bone

Shoulder blade

1st to 7th pairs of
ribs are true ribs, joined
to the breastbone by
cartilage ("costal
cartilage")

Costal cartilage

8th to 10th pairs
of ribs are false ribs,
joined to the ribs
above at the front

Vertebrae

11th and 12th pairs of ribs
are floating ribs, not joined
at the front

COMPLETE CASING
Medieval suits of armor were
designed to give complete
protection. Suits were very
strong around the chest, since
here are sited the heart
and lungs, those most
vital of organs.

**RIBBED
FOR STRENGTH**
In the invertebrate
world, the cockle's
ribbed shells form a
virtually impenetrable
casing around the soft
animal. This type of
double shell is called a
bivalve shell.

SPARE RIB
Biblical accounts describe Eve,
the first woman, as being
created from Adam's
spare rib. But most men,
and women have 12
complete pairs of ribs.
Occasionally a
man or woman
has 11 or 13
pairs - an
oddity of
nature.

Human hip bones

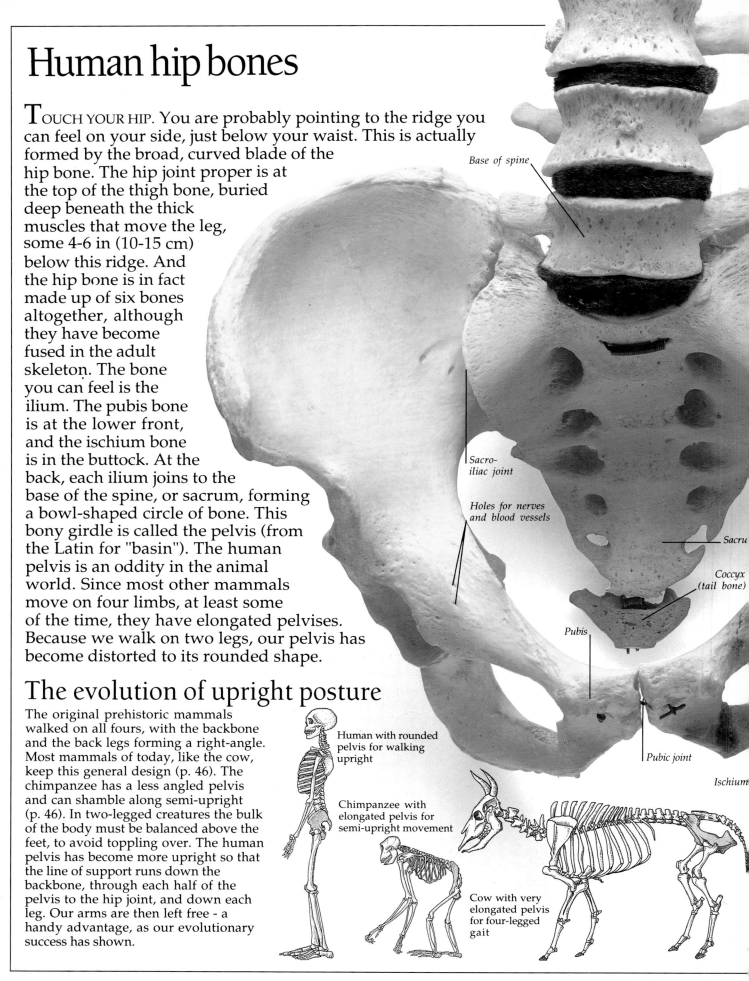

T OUCH YOUR HIP. You are probably pointing to the ridge you can feel on your side, just below your waist. This is actually formed by the broad, curved blade of the hip bone. The hip joint proper is at the top of the thigh bone, buried deep beneath the thick muscles that move the leg, some 4-6 in (10-15 cm) below this ridge. And the hip bone is in fact made up of six bones altogether, although they have become fused in the adult skeleton. The bone you can feel is the ilium. The pubis bone is at the lower front, and the ischium bone is in the buttock. At the back, each ilium joins to the base of the spine, or sacrum, forming a bowl-shaped circle of bone. This bony girdle is called the pelvis (from the Latin for "basin"). The human pelvis is an oddity in the animal world. Since most other mammals move on four limbs, at least some of the time, they have elongated pelvises. Because we walk on two legs, our pelvis has become distorted to its rounded shape.

Base of spine

Sacro-iliac joint

Holes for nerves and blood vessels

Sacru

Coccyx (tail bone)

Pubis

Pubic joint

Ischium

The evolution of upright posture

The original prehistoric mammals walked on all fours, with the backbone and the back legs forming a right-angle. Most mammals of today, like the cow, keep this general design (p. 46). The chimpanzee has a less angled pelvis and can shamble along semi-upright (p. 46). In two-legged creatures the bulk of the body must be balanced above the feet, to avoid toppling over. The human pelvis has become more upright so that the line of support runs down the backbone, through each half of the pelvis to the hip joint, and down each leg. Our arms are then left free - a handy advantage, as our evolutionary success has shown.

Human with rounded pelvis for walking upright

Chimpanzee with elongated pelvis for semi-upright movement

Cow with very elongated pelvis for four-legged gait

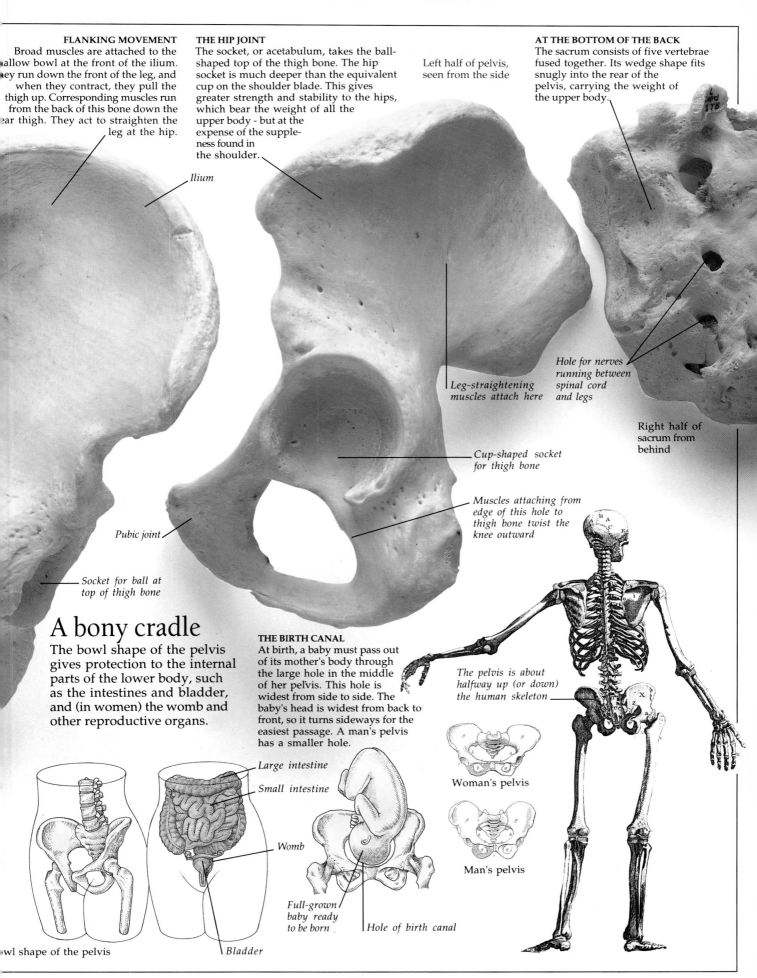

FLANKING MOVEMENT
Broad muscles are attached to the shallow bowl at the front of the ilium. They run down the front of the leg, and when they contract, they pull the thigh up. Corresponding muscles run from the back of this bone down the rear thigh. They act to straighten the leg at the hip.

THE HIP JOINT
The socket, or acetabulum, takes the ball-shaped top of the thigh bone. The hip socket is much deeper than the equivalent cup on the shoulder blade. This gives greater strength and stability to the hips, which bear the weight of all the upper body - but at the expense of the suppleness found in the shoulder.

Left half of pelvis, seen from the side

AT THE BOTTOM OF THE BACK
The sacrum consists of five vertebrae fused together. Its wedge shape fits snugly into the rear of the pelvis, carrying the weight of the upper body.

Ilium

Leg-straightening muscles attach here

Hole for nerves running between spinal cord and legs

Right half of sacrum from behind

Cup-shaped socket for thigh bone

Muscles attaching from edge of this hole to thigh bone twist the knee outward

Pubic joint

Socket for ball at top of thigh bone

A bony cradle

The bowl shape of the pelvis gives protection to the internal parts of the lower body, such as the intestines and bladder, and (in women) the womb and other reproductive organs.

THE BIRTH CANAL
At birth, a baby must pass out of its mother's body through the large hole in the middle of her pelvis. This hole is widest from side to side. The baby's head is widest from back to front, so it turns sideways for the easiest passage. A man's pelvis has a smaller hole.

The pelvis is about halfway up (or down) the human skeleton

Large intestine

Small intestine

Womb

Woman's pelvis

Man's pelvis

Full-grown baby ready to be born

Hole of birth canal

wl shape of the pelvis

Bladder

45

Animal hip bones

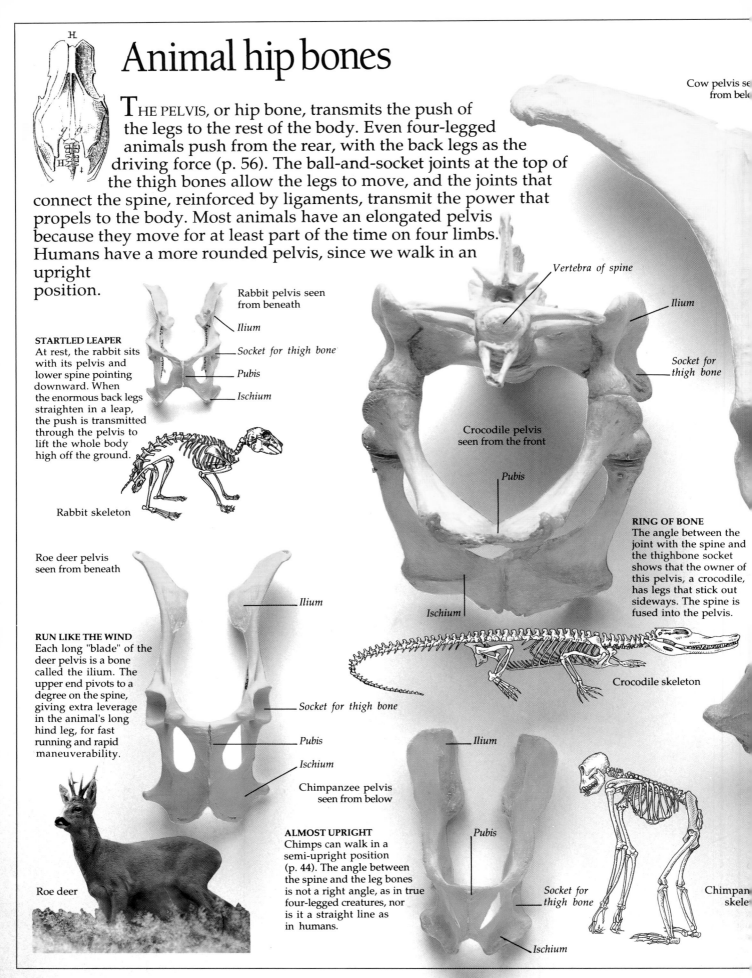

THE PELVIS, or hip bone, transmits the push of the legs to the rest of the body. Even four-legged animals push from the rear, with the back legs as the driving force (p. 56). The ball-and-socket joints at the top of the thigh bones allow the legs to move, and the joints that connect the spine, reinforced by ligaments, transmit the power that propels to the body. Most animals have an elongated pelvis because they move for at least part of the time on four limbs. Humans have a more rounded pelvis, since we walk in an upright position.

Cow pelvis se[en] from belo[w]

STARTLED LEAPER
At rest, the rabbit sits with its pelvis and lower spine pointing downward. When the enormous back legs straighten in a leap, the push is transmitted through the pelvis to lift the whole body high off the ground.

Rabbit pelvis seen from beneath

Ilium

Socket for thigh bone

Pubis

Ischium

Rabbit skeleton

Vertebra of spine

Ilium

Socket for thigh bone

Crocodile pelvis seen from the front

Pubis

Ischium

RING OF BONE
The angle between the joint with the spine and the thighbone socket shows that the owner of this pelvis, a crocodile, has legs that stick out sideways. The spine is fused into the pelvis.

Crocodile skeleton

Roe deer pelvis seen from beneath

Ilium

RUN LIKE THE WIND
Each long "blade" of the deer pelvis is a bone called the ilium. The upper end pivots to a degree on the spine, giving extra leverage in the animal's long hind leg, for fast running and rapid maneuverability.

Socket for thigh bone

Pubis

Ischium

Chimpanzee pelvis seen from below

Ilium

Roe deer

ALMOST UPRIGHT
Chimps can walk in a semi-upright position (p. 44). The angle between the spine and the leg bones is not a right angle, as in true four-legged creatures, nor is it a straight line as in humans.

Pubis

Socket for thigh bone

Chimpan[zee] skele[ton]

Ischium

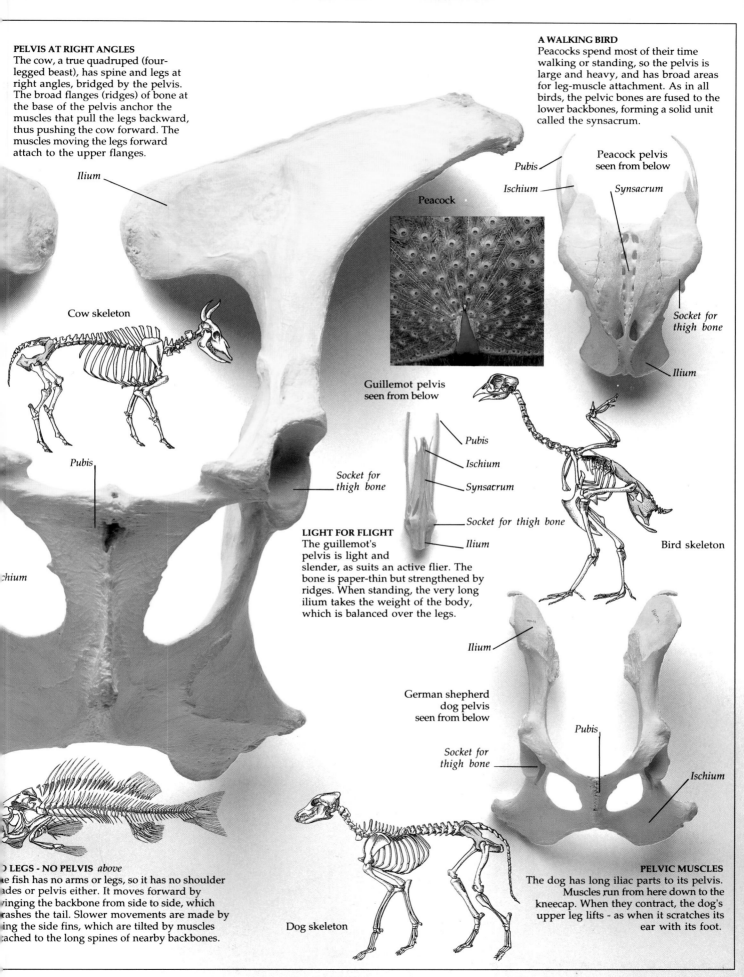

PELVIS AT RIGHT ANGLES
The cow, a true quadruped (four-legged beast), has spine and legs at right angles, bridged by the pelvis. The broad flanges (ridges) of bone at the base of the pelvis anchor the muscles that pull the legs backward, thus pushing the cow forward. The muscles moving the legs forward attach to the upper flanges.

Ilium

Cow skeleton

Pubis

Ischium

A WALKING BIRD
Peacocks spend most of their time walking or standing, so the pelvis is large and heavy, and has broad areas for leg-muscle attachment. As in all birds, the pelvic bones are fused to the lower backbones, forming a solid unit called the synsacrum.

Peacock

Peacock pelvis seen from below

Pubis

Ischium

Synsacrum

Socket for thigh bone

Ilium

Guillemot pelvis seen from below

Pubis

Ischium

Synsacrum

Socket for thigh bone

Ilium

Socket for thigh bone

LIGHT FOR FLIGHT
The guillemot's pelvis is light and slender, as suits an active flier. The bone is paper-thin but strengthened by ridges. When standing, the very long ilium takes the weight of the body, which is balanced over the legs.

Bird skeleton

Ilium

German shepherd dog pelvis seen from below

Socket for thigh bone

Pubis

Ischium

NO LEGS - NO PELVIS *above*
The fish has no arms or legs, so it has no shoulder blades or pelvis either. It moves forward by swinging the backbone from side to side, which lashes the tail. Slower movements are made by using the side fins, which are tilted by muscles attached to the long spines of nearby backbones.

Dog skeleton

PELVIC MUSCLES
The dog has long iliac parts to its pelvis. Muscles run from here down to the kneecap. When they contract, the dog's upper leg lifts - as when it scratches its ear with its foot.

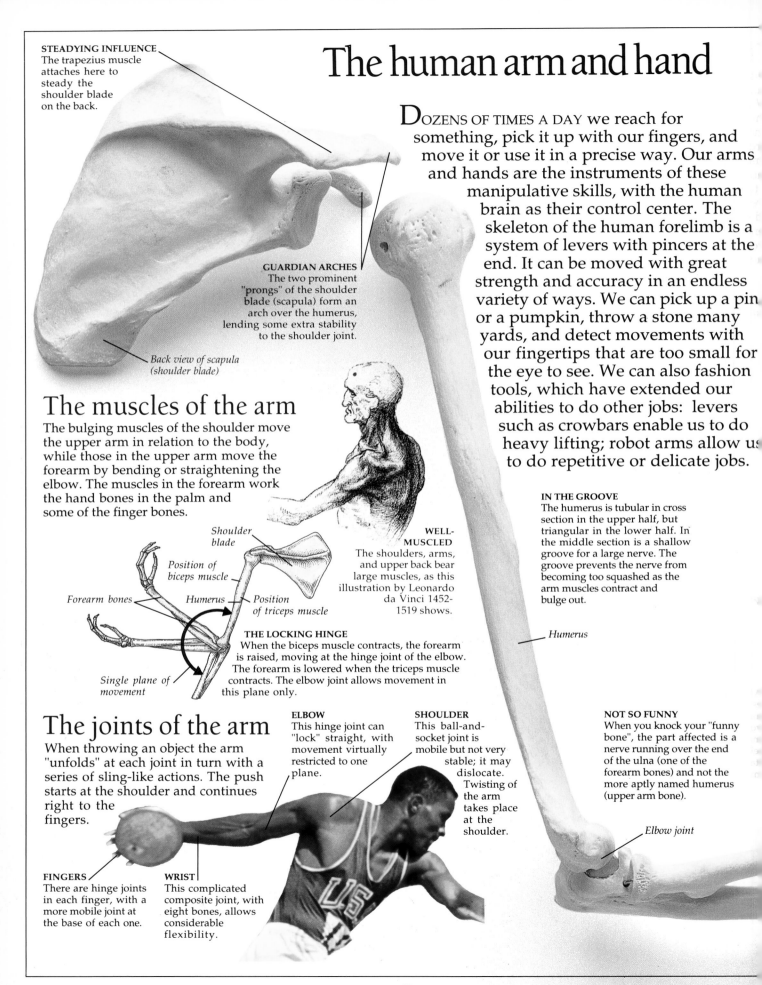

The human arm and hand

STEADYING INFLUENCE
The trapezius muscle attaches here to steady the shoulder blade on the back.

GUARDIAN ARCHES
The two prominent "prongs" of the shoulder blade (scapula) form an arch over the humerus, lending some extra stability to the shoulder joint.

Back view of scapula (shoulder blade)

DOZENS OF TIMES A DAY we reach for something, pick it up with our fingers, and move it or use it in a precise way. Our arms and hands are the instruments of these manipulative skills, with the human brain as their control center. The skeleton of the human forelimb is a system of levers with pincers at the end. It can be moved with great strength and accuracy in an endless variety of ways. We can pick up a pin or a pumpkin, throw a stone many yards, and detect movements with our fingertips that are too small for the eye to see. We can also fashion tools, which have extended our abilities to do other jobs: levers such as crowbars enable us to do heavy lifting; robot arms allow us to do repetitive or delicate jobs.

The muscles of the arm

The bulging muscles of the shoulder move the upper arm in relation to the body, while those in the upper arm move the forearm by bending or straightening the elbow. The muscles in the forearm work the hand bones in the palm and some of the finger bones.

Shoulder blade

Position of biceps muscle

Forearm bones

Humerus

Position of triceps muscle

Single plane of movement

WELL-MUSCLED
The shoulders, arms, and upper back bear large muscles, as this illustration by Leonardo da Vinci 1452-1519 shows.

THE LOCKING HINGE
When the biceps muscle contracts, the forearm is raised, moving at the hinge joint of the elbow. The forearm is lowered when the triceps muscle contracts. The elbow joint allows movement in this plane only.

IN THE GROOVE
The humerus is tubular in cross section in the upper half, but triangular in the lower half. In the middle section is a shallow groove for a large nerve. The groove prevents the nerve from becoming too squashed as the arm muscles contract and bulge out.

Humerus

The joints of the arm

When throwing an object the arm "unfolds" at each joint in turn with a series of sling-like actions. The push starts at the shoulder and continues right to the fingers.

ELBOW
This hinge joint can "lock" straight, with movement virtually restricted to one plane.

SHOULDER
This ball-and-socket joint is mobile but not very stable; it may dislocate. Twisting of the arm takes place at the shoulder.

NOT SO FUNNY
When you knock your "funny bone", the part affected is a nerve running over the end of the ulna (one of the forearm bones) and not the more aptly named humerus (upper arm bone).

Elbow joint

FINGERS
There are hinge joints in each finger, with a more mobile joint at the base of each one.

WRIST
This complicated composite joint, with eight bones, allows considerable flexibility.

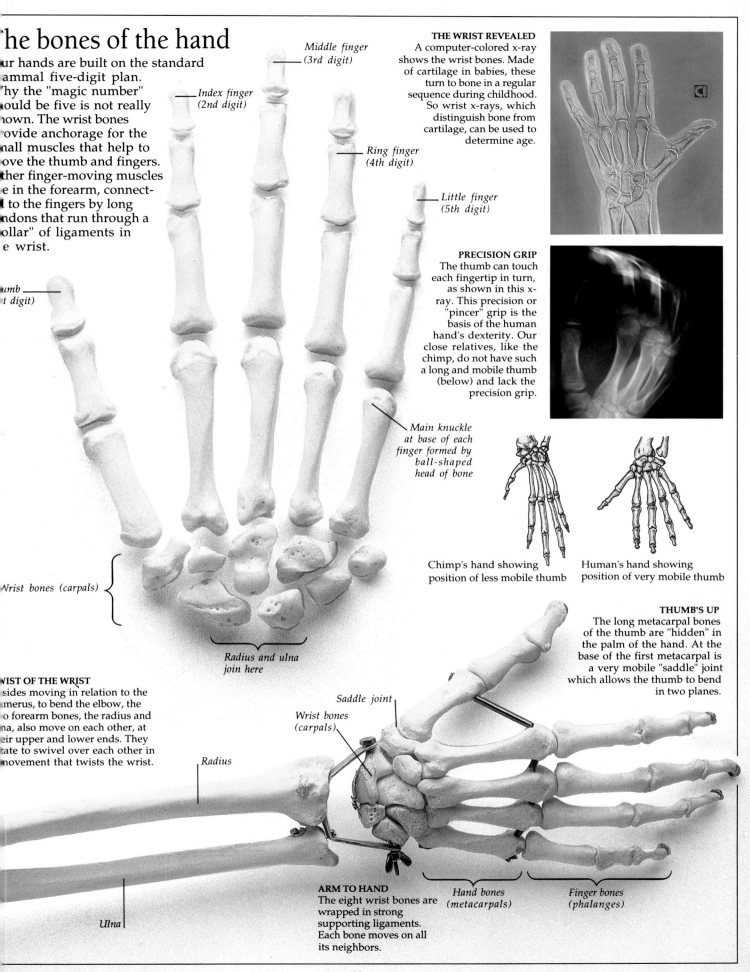

The bones of the hand

Our hands are built on the standard mammal five-digit plan. Why the "magic number" should be five is not really known. The wrist bones provide anchorage for the small muscles that help to move the thumb and fingers. Other finger-moving muscles are in the forearm, connected to the fingers by long tendons that run through a "collar" of ligaments in the wrist.

Thumb
(1st digit)

Index finger
(2nd digit)

Middle finger
(3rd digit)

Ring finger
(4th digit)

Little finger
(5th digit)

Main knuckle at base of each finger formed by ball-shaped head of bone

Wrist bones (carpals)

Radius and ulna join here

TWIST OF THE WRIST

Besides moving in relation to the humerus, to bend the elbow, the two forearm bones, the radius and ulna, also move on each other, at their upper and lower ends. They rotate to swivel over each other in a movement that twists the wrist.

Radius

Ulna

THE WRIST REVEALED

A computer-colored x-ray shows the wrist bones. Made of cartilage in babies, these turn to bone in a regular sequence during childhood. So wrist x-rays, which distinguish bone from cartilage, can be used to determine age.

PRECISION GRIP

The thumb can touch each fingertip in turn, as shown in this x-ray. This precision or "pincer" grip is the basis of the human hand's dexterity. Our close relatives, like the chimp, do not have such a long and mobile thumb (below) and lack the precision grip.

Chimp's hand showing position of less mobile thumb

Human's hand showing position of very mobile thumb

THUMB'S UP

The long metacarpal bones of the thumb are "hidden" in the palm of the hand. At the base of the first metacarpal is a very mobile "saddle" joint which allows the thumb to bend in two planes.

Saddle joint

Wrist bones (carpals)

ARM TO HAND

The eight wrist bones are wrapped in strong supporting ligaments. Each bone moves on all its neighbors.

Hand bones (metacarpals)

Finger bones (phalanges)

Arms, wings, and flippers

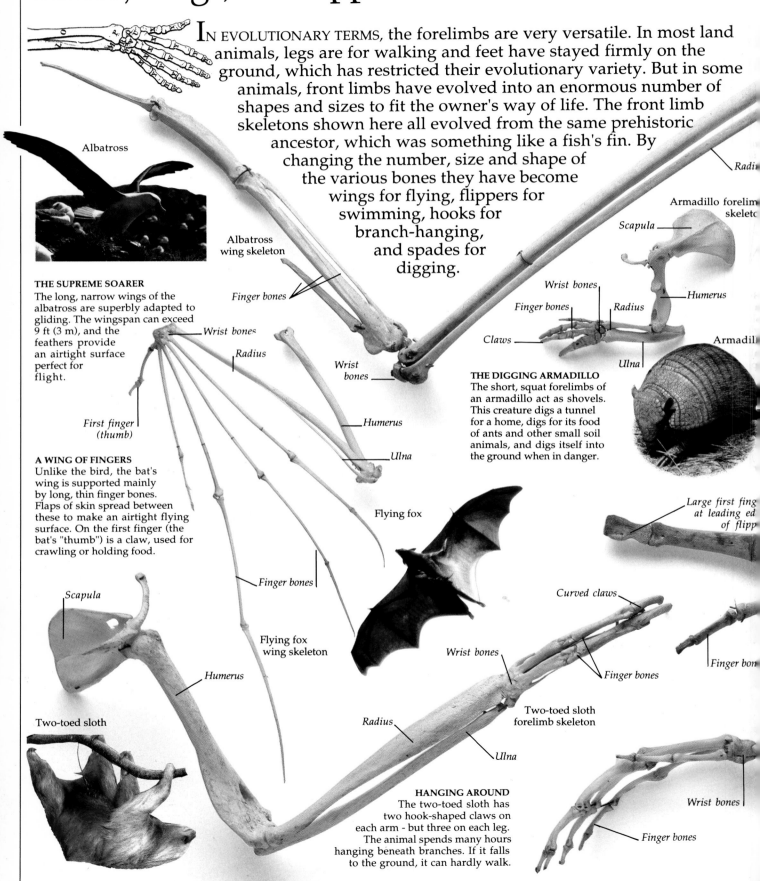

IN EVOLUTIONARY TERMS, the forelimbs are very versatile. In most land animals, legs are for walking and feet have stayed firmly on the ground, which has restricted their evolutionary variety. But in some animals, front limbs have evolved into an enormous number of shapes and sizes to fit the owner's way of life. The front limb skeletons shown here all evolved from the same prehistoric ancestor, which was something like a fish's fin. By changing the number, size and shape of the various bones they have become wings for flying, flippers for swimming, hooks for branch-hanging, and spades for digging.

Albatross

Albatross wing skeleton

Finger bones

Wrist bones

Radius

First finger (thumb)

Wrist bones

Radius

Wrist bones

Humerus

Ulna

Radi...

Armadillo forelimb skeleto...

Scapula

Wrist bones

Finger bones

Radius

Humerus

Claws

Ulna

Armadil...

THE SUPREME SOARER
The long, narrow wings of the albatross are superbly adapted to gliding. The wingspan can exceed 9 ft (3 m), and the feathers provide an airtight surface perfect for flight.

A WING OF FINGERS
Unlike the bird, the bat's wing is supported mainly by long, thin finger bones. Flaps of skin spread between these to make an airtight flying surface. On the first finger (the bat's "thumb") is a claw, used for crawling or holding food.

THE DIGGING ARMADILLO
The short, squat forelimbs of an armadillo act as shovels. This creature digs a tunnel for a home, digs for its food of ants and other small soil animals, and digs itself into the ground when in danger.

Flying fox

Large first fing... at leading ed... of flipp...

Scapula

Finger bones

Flying fox wing skeleton

Humerus

Two-toed sloth

Curved claws

Wrist bones

Finger bones

Finger bon...

Two-toed sloth forelimb skeleton

Radius

Ulna

Wrist bones

Finger bones

HANGING AROUND
The two-toed sloth has two hook-shaped claws on each arm - but three on each leg. The animal spends many hours hanging beneath branches. If it falls to the ground, it can hardly walk.

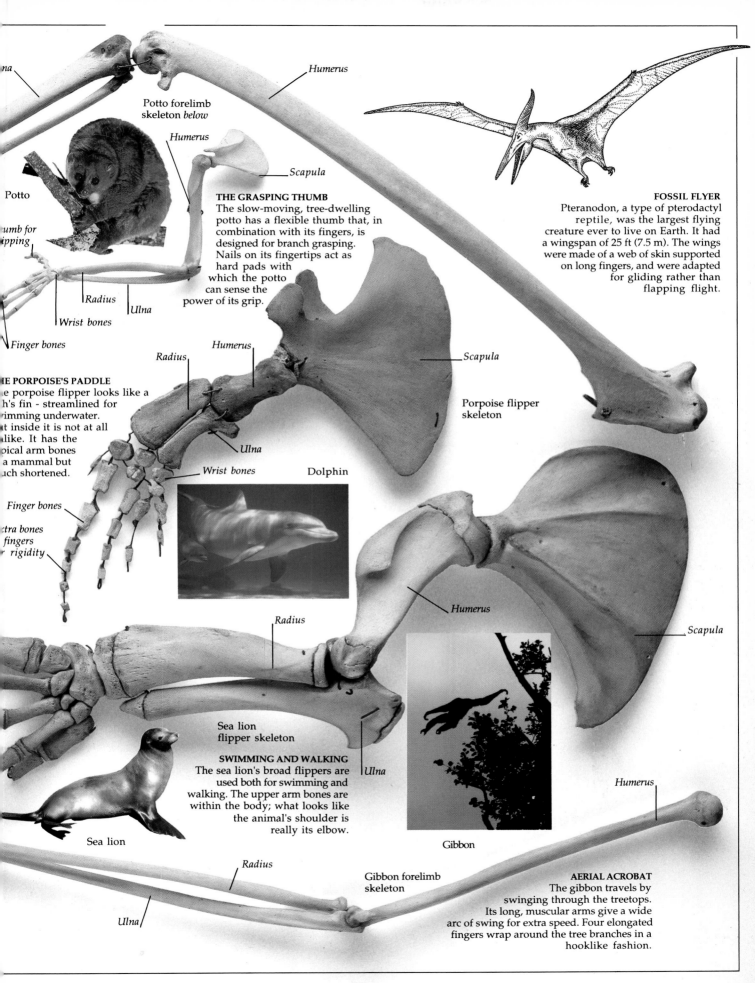

Humerus

Potto forelimb
skeleton *below*

Humerus

Scapula

na

Potto

*umb for
ipping*

Radius

Ulna

Wrist bones

Finger bones

THE GRASPING THUMB
The slow-moving, tree-dwelling
potto has a flexible thumb that, in
combination with its fingers, is
designed for branch grasping.
Nails on its fingertips act as
hard pads with
which the potto
can sense the
power of its grip.

FOSSIL FLYER
Pteranodon, a type of pterodactyl
reptile, was the largest flying
creature ever to live on Earth. It had
a wingspan of 25 ft (7.5 m). The wings
were made of a web of skin supported
on long fingers, and were adapted
for gliding rather than
flapping flight.

IE PORPOISE'S PADDLE
e porpoise flipper looks like a
h's fin - streamlined for
imming underwater.
t inside it is not at all
like. It has the
pical arm bones
a mammal but
ch shortened.

Radius

Humerus

Scapula

Porpoise flipper
skeleton

Ulna

Wrist bones

Dolphin

Finger bones

*tra bones
fingers
r rigidity*

Radius

Humerus

Scapula

Sea lion
flipper skeleton

Ulna

SWIMMING AND WALKING
The sea lion's broad flippers are
used both for swimming and
walking. The upper arm bones are
within the body; what looks like
the animal's shoulder is
really its elbow.

Sea lion

Gibbon

Humerus

Radius

Gibbon forelimb
skeleton

AERIAL ACROBAT
The gibbon travels by
swinging through the treetops.
Its long, muscular arms give a wide
arc of swing for extra speed. Four elongated
fingers wrap around the tree branches in a
hooklike fashion.

Ulna

Animal shoulder blades

Red

Red fox shoulder blade

FROM THE OUTSIDE, the four limbs of a four-legged animal look much the same. But inside, the skeleton reveals many differences. The back legs are designed mainly for moving the whole body forward when walking, running, or jumping (p. 56). The front legs, on the other hand, do various jobs. They cushion the body when landing after a leap; they may move and hold food or objects; and they can strike at prey or enemies. So they need to be more flexible. The key to their wider range of movement is the shoulder blade, or scapula. This triangle of bone connects to the body chiefly by muscles that run to the backbone and ribs, and which can tilt the scapula at many angles. And it links to the forelimb by a ball-and-socket joint, giving even greater flexibility.

ON THE TROT
The fox's broad shoulder blade has a large surface area for muscle anchorage, indicating that it moves for much of the time on all fours. Foxes may also dig for food with their front legs.

Collared peccary shoulder blade

STIFF-LEGGED PIG
The long, narrow shoulder blade of the collared peccary, a type of pig, is swung forward and back by the muscles connecting it to the body. The legs are relatively short and thin, resulting in a rather stiff-legged walk.

Pig skeleton

Wallaby shoulder blade

Beaver holding twig it is gnawing

DAM BUILDER
The beaver's smallish shoulder blade shows that its short front limbs are not weight carriers. They are manipulators for holding food and prodding twigs and mud into dams.

CROUCHING TO DRINK
A Siberian tiger lowers itself over a pool to drink. Its spine is lowered between its front legs, and the shoulder blades show clearly on each side of the body.

Beaver shoulder blade

TWO-LEGGED HOPPING
The forelimbs of a kangaroo or wallaby take no part in its fast hopping movements. They are used to fight and play, to pick up food, and to lean on when grazing.

Kangaroo skeleton

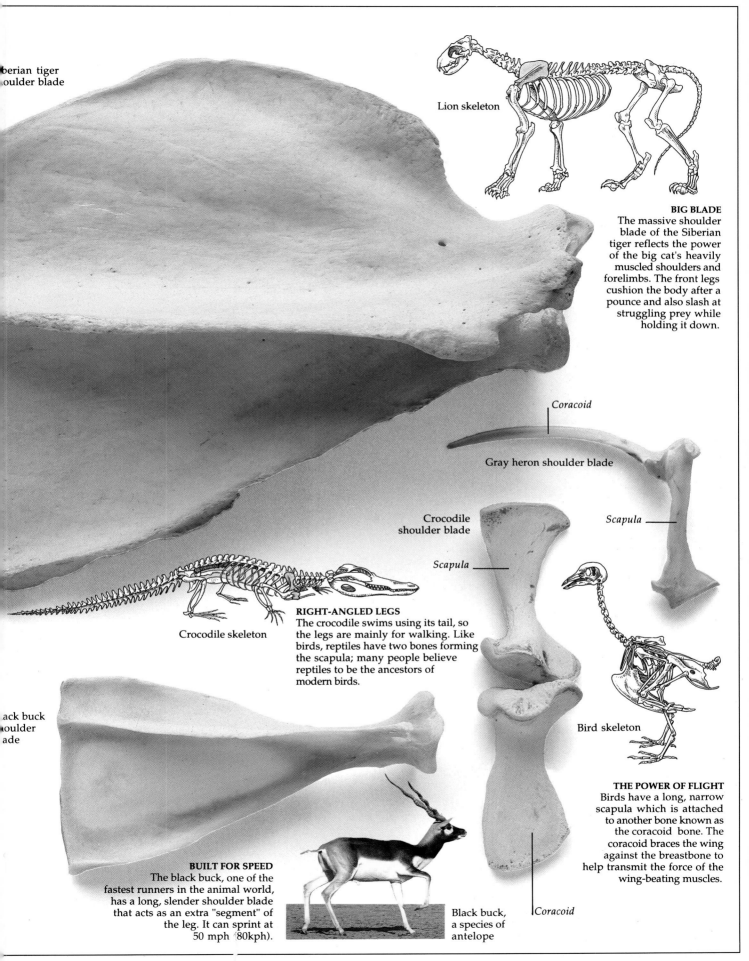

Siberian tiger
shoulder blade

Lion skeleton

BIG BLADE
The massive shoulder blade of the Siberian tiger reflects the power of the big cat's heavily muscled shoulders and forelimbs. The front legs cushion the body after a pounce and also slash at struggling prey while holding it down.

Coracoid

Gray heron shoulder blade

Crocodile
shoulder blade

Scapula

Scapula

Scapula

RIGHT-ANGLED LEGS
The crocodile swims using its tail, so the legs are mainly for walking. Like birds, reptiles have two bones forming the scapula; many people believe reptiles to be the ancestors of modern birds.

Crocodile skeleton

Bird skeleton

ack buck
houlder
ade

THE POWER OF FLIGHT
Birds have a long, narrow scapula which is attached to another bone known as the coracoid bone. The coracoid braces the wing against the breastbone to help transmit the force of the wing-beating muscles.

BUILT FOR SPEED
The black buck, one of the fastest runners in the animal world, has a long, slender shoulder blade that acts as an extra "segment" of the leg. It can sprint at 50 mph (80kph).

Black buck,
a species of
antelope

Coracoid

The human leg and foot

Head of thigh bone

Thigh bone (femur)

W E ARE SO used to standing and watching the world go by that we are not usually aware of what an amazing balancing feat this is. Other animals may be able to stand on their back limbs temporarily, but they usually topple over after a few seconds. We can maintain a fully upright, two-legged posture for hours, leaving our arms and hands free for other tasks. Compared to the arm (p. 48), the bones of the human leg are thick and strong, to carry the body's weight. We do not walk on our toes, like many creatures (p. 56). Our feet are broad and also long, for good stability, and our toes are much smaller than in most other animals. Small muscle adjustments take place continuously in the neck, arms, back, and legs, keeping our weight over our feet. Walking requires the coordination and contraction of dozens of muscles. It has been called "controlled falling": the body tilts forwards, so that it begins to tip over, only to be saved from falling by moving a foot forward.

THE HEAD OF THE LEG
The thigh bone is the largest single bone in the body. At its top end, or "head", it is reinforced by ridges that anchor powerful leg-moving muscles.

LONG, YET STRONG
In accordance with go engineering design, th shaft of the thigh bo is long and tubelike. is subjected to fewer stresses and strains along its length than at the ends.

SWINGING AR
As you walk, the arm on one s swings forward as the on that side swings back. T two movements partly cancel ea other out, keeping the body's weig mostly in the cent

The muscles and joints of the leg

The muscles at the hip, thigh, and calf move the limbs at the joints. Those at the hip swing the leg forward and backward at the hip joint, as when walking. The muscles at the back of the thigh bend the knee at its hinge joint. Those in the calf straighten the foot at the ankle joint.

THE I
This ball-and-socket jo combines great streng with some mobility. T ball of the thigh bone at an angle to the sh so as to come mo directly under t middle of the bod

THE KN
This joint works like a hin its main movements be forward and backward cannot cope with too mu twisting, when it m become damage

MUSCLES FOR MOVING THE LEG
This rear view of the legs shows all the muscles important in movement.

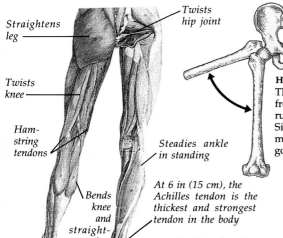

Straightens leg

Twists knee

Ham-string tendons

Bends knee and straightens foot

Twists hip joint

Steadies ankle in standing

At 6 in (15 cm), the Achilles tendon is the thickest and strongest tendon in the body

Twists sole of foot inwards

HIP LIMITS
The hip moves easily from front to back for running and walking. Side-to-side move-ment is limited but good for suddenly changing direction.

THE ANK
Seven bones make up ankle, a composite joi Each bone moves a lit in relation to its neig bors, giving gr overall strength wi limited flexibili

279
GUINNE
279

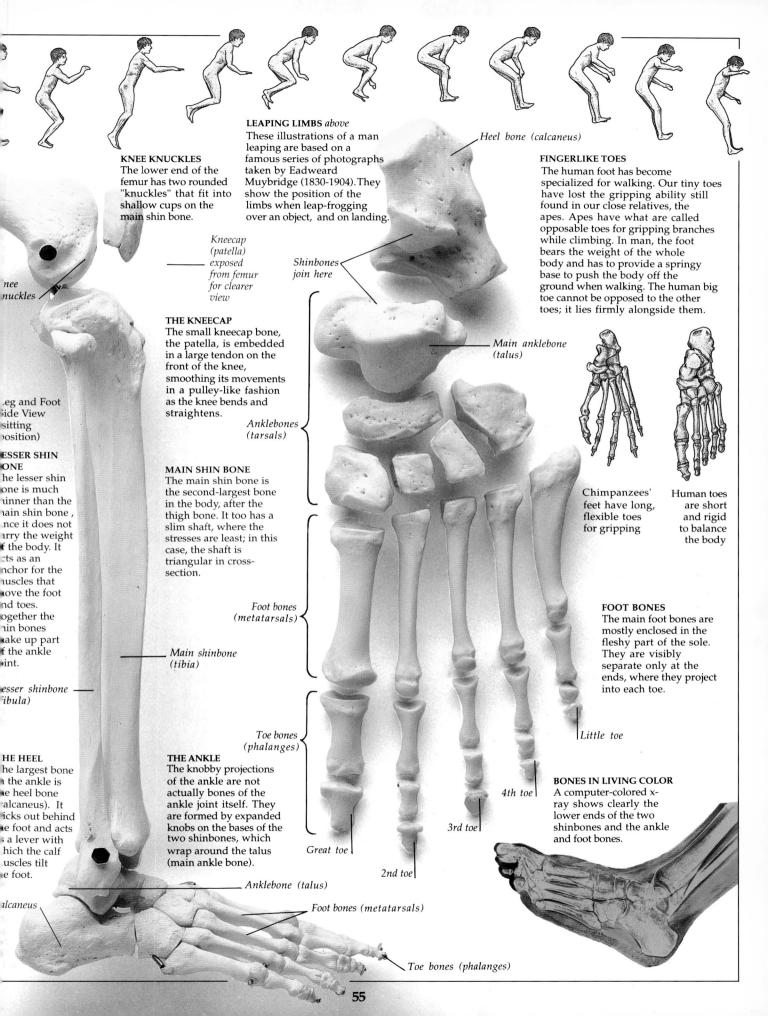

KNEE KNUCKLES
The lower end of the femur has two rounded "knuckles" that fit into shallow cups on the main shin bone.

LEAPING LIMBS *above*
These illustrations of a man leaping are based on a famous series of photographs taken by Eadweard Muybridge (1830-1904). They show the position of the limbs when leap-frogging over an object, and on landing.

Kneecap (patella) exposed from femur for clearer view

Shinbones join here

THE KNEECAP
The small kneecap bone, the patella, is embedded in a large tendon on the front of the knee, smoothing its movements in a pulley-like fashion as the knee bends and straightens.

Anklebones (tarsals)

MAIN SHIN BONE
The main shin bone is the second-largest bone in the body, after the thigh bone. It too has a slim shaft, where the stresses are least; in this case, the shaft is triangular in cross-section.

Heel bone (calcaneus)

FINGERLIKE TOES
The human foot has become specialized for walking. Our tiny toes have lost the gripping ability still found in our close relatives, the apes. Apes have what are called opposable toes for gripping branches while climbing. In man, the foot bears the weight of the whole body and has to provide a springy base to push the body off the ground when walking. The human big toe cannot be opposed to the other toes; it lies firmly alongside them.

Main anklebone (talus)

Chimpanzees' feet have long, flexible toes for gripping

Human toes are short and rigid to balance the body

FOOT BONES
The main foot bones are mostly enclosed in the fleshy part of the sole. They are visibly separate only at the ends, where they project into each toe.

Foot bones (metatarsals)

Main shinbone (tibia)

Little toe

Leg and Foot Side View (sitting position)

LESSER SHIN BONE
The lesser shin bone is much thinner than the main shin bone, since it does not carry the weight of the body. It acts as an anchor for the muscles that move the foot and toes. Together the shin bones make up part of the ankle joint.

Lesser shinbone (fibula)

Toe bones (phalanges)

THE ANKLE
The knobby projections of the ankle are not actually bones of the ankle joint itself. They are formed by expanded knobs on the bases of the two shinbones, which wrap around the talus (main ankle bone).

4th toe

3rd toe

BONES IN LIVING COLOR
A computer-colored x-ray shows clearly the lower ends of the two shinbones and the ankle and foot bones.

THE HEEL
The largest bone in the ankle is the heel bone (calcaneus). It sticks out behind the foot and acts as a lever with which the calf muscles tilt the foot.

calcaneus

Great toe

2nd toe

Anklebone (talus)

Foot bones (metatarsals)

Toe bones (phalanges)

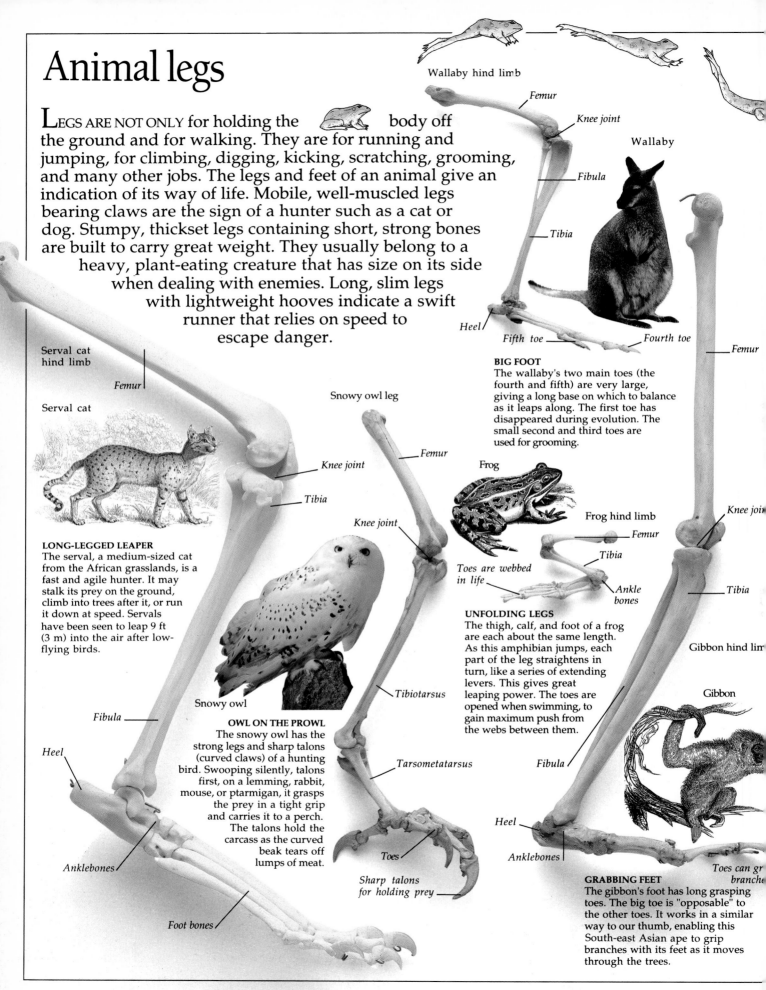

Animal legs

LEGS ARE NOT ONLY for holding the body off the ground and for walking. They are for running and jumping, for climbing, digging, kicking, scratching, grooming, and many other jobs. The legs and feet of an animal give an indication of its way of life. Mobile, well-muscled legs bearing claws are the sign of a hunter such as a cat or dog. Stumpy, thickset legs containing short, strong bones are built to carry great weight. They usually belong to a heavy, plant-eating creature that has size on its side when dealing with enemies. Long, slim legs with lightweight hooves indicate a swift runner that relies on speed to escape danger.

Wallaby hind limb

Femur

Knee joint

Wallaby

Fibula

Tibia

Heel

Fifth toe

Fourth toe

Femur

BIG FOOT
The wallaby's two main toes (the fourth and fifth) are very large, giving a long base on which to balance as it leaps along. The first toe has disappeared during evolution. The small second and third toes are used for grooming.

Serval cat hind limb

Femur

Serval cat

Snowy owl leg

Femur

Knee joint

Tibia

Frog

Knee joint

Frog hind limb

Femur

Tibia

Toes are webbed in life

Ankle bones

Knee joi

Tibia

LONG-LEGGED LEAPER
The serval, a medium-sized cat from the African grasslands, is a fast and agile hunter. It may stalk its prey on the ground, climb into trees after it, or run it down at speed. Servals have been seen to leap 9 ft (3 m) into the air after low-flying birds.

Fibula

Heel

Anklebones

Foot bones

Snowy owl

Tibiotarsus

OWL ON THE PROWL
The snowy owl has the strong legs and sharp talons (curved claws) of a hunting bird. Swooping silently, talons first, on a lemming, rabbit, mouse, or ptarmigan, it grasps the prey in a tight grip and carries it to a perch. The talons hold the carcass as the curved beak tears off lumps of meat.

Tarsometatarsus

Toes

Sharp talons for holding prey

UNFOLDING LEGS
The thigh, calf, and foot of a frog are each about the same length. As this amphibian jumps, each part of the leg straightens in turn, like a series of extending levers. This gives great leaping power. The toes are opened when swimming, to gain maximum push from the webs between them.

Fibula

Gibbon hind lim

Gibbon

Heel

Anklebones

Toes can gr
branche

GRABBING FEET
The gibbon's foot has long grasping toes. The big toe is "opposable" to the other toes. It works in a similar way to our thumb, enabling this South-east Asian ape to grip branches with its feet as it moves through the trees.

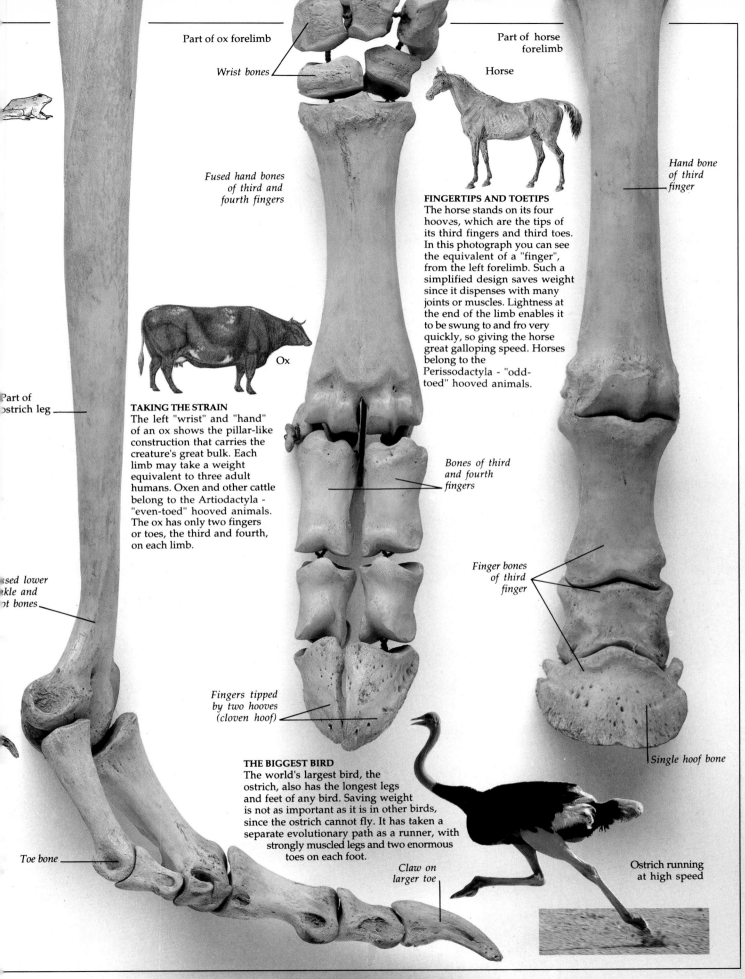

Part of ox forelimb

Wrist bones

Part of horse forelimb

Horse

Fused hand bones of third and fourth fingers

Hand bone of third finger

FINGERTIPS AND TOETIPS
The horse stands on its four hooves, which are the tips of its third fingers and third toes. In this photograph you can see the equivalent of a "finger", from the left forelimb. Such a simplified design saves weight since it dispenses with many joints or muscles. Lightness at the end of the limb enables it to be swung to and fro very quickly, so giving the horse great galloping speed. Horses belong to the Perissodactyla - "odd-toed" hooved animals.

Ox

Part of ostrich leg

TAKING THE STRAIN
The left "wrist" and "hand" of an ox shows the pillar-like construction that carries the creature's great bulk. Each limb may take a weight equivalent to three adult humans. Oxen and other cattle belong to the Artiodactyla - "even-toed" hooved animals. The ox has only two fingers or toes, the third and fourth, on each limb.

Bones of third and fourth fingers

used lower kle and t bones

Finger bones of third finger

Fingers tipped by two hooves (cloven hoof)

Single hoof bone

THE BIGGEST BIRD
The world's largest bird, the ostrich, also has the longest legs and feet of any bird. Saving weight is not as important as it is in other birds, since the ostrich cannot fly. It has taken a separate evolutionary path as a runner, with strongly muscled legs and two enormous toes on each foot.

Toe bone

Claw on larger toe

Ostrich running at high speed

The largest and smallest bones

Giant Hugo

BONES, LIKE OTHER PARTS OF THE BODY, vary in exact size and shape from person to person. Tall people have longer bones than shorter people, especially in the legs, where the thigh bone makes up about one-quarter of the body's height. Most of these variations in bone length are slight, however, with the average man being taller than the average woman. Occasionally a disease or inherited condition affects development of bones as the baby grows in the womb. Or bone growth during childhood, which is controlled mainly by hormones, may be affected by disease, illness, or a poor diet. The result is an unusually tall or small person.

Reconstructed fossil skeleton of Iguanodon

ANIMAL GIANTS
Dinosaurs, the largest land animals ever, had gigantic bones. The thigh bone of this Iguanodon (p. 12) was 4 ft 3 in (1.3 m) long. Some dinosaur arm bones were nearly 9 ft (3 m) long!

VERY TALL
Gigantism is caused by a hormone condition that makes the bones grow very fast. Authentic records give the tallest man ever as American Robert Wadlow at 8 ft 11 in (2.7 m). Above is another famous American, Giant Hugo.

VERY SMALL
The smallest humans measure about 2 ft to 2 ft 6 in (60 cm to 75 cm). One of the best-known midgets, shown here with his midget wife, was Charles Stratton ("General Tom Thumb") who was 3 ft 4 in (1.02 m) short.

"Tom Thumb" at his wedding

The size of the thighs

This array of 10 thigh bones (femurs) shows the enormous size differences within the mammal group. In general, fast-moving animals have long, slender leg bones in relation to their body size. The seal's femurs are a special case: they are within the body, and this animal swims using its back flippers, which contain its shin and feet bones.

RABBIT
Body length - 12 in (30 cm)
Femur length - 3 in (8 cm)

HEDGEHOG
Body length - 8 in (20 cm)
Femur length - 1.6 in (4 cm)

SEAL
Body length - 5 ft (1.6 m)
Femur length - 4.5 in (11 cm)

DOG (BASSET HOUND)
Body length - 2 ft 4 in (70 cm)
Femur length - 4.5 in (11 cm)

CAT *left*
Body length - 1 ft 8 in (50 cm)
Femur length - 5 in (12 cm)

SHEEP *left*
Body length - 4 ft 8 in (1.4 m)
Femur length - 7 in (18 cm)

ROE DEER *right*
Body length - 3 ft (1 m)
Femur length - 7 in (18 cm)

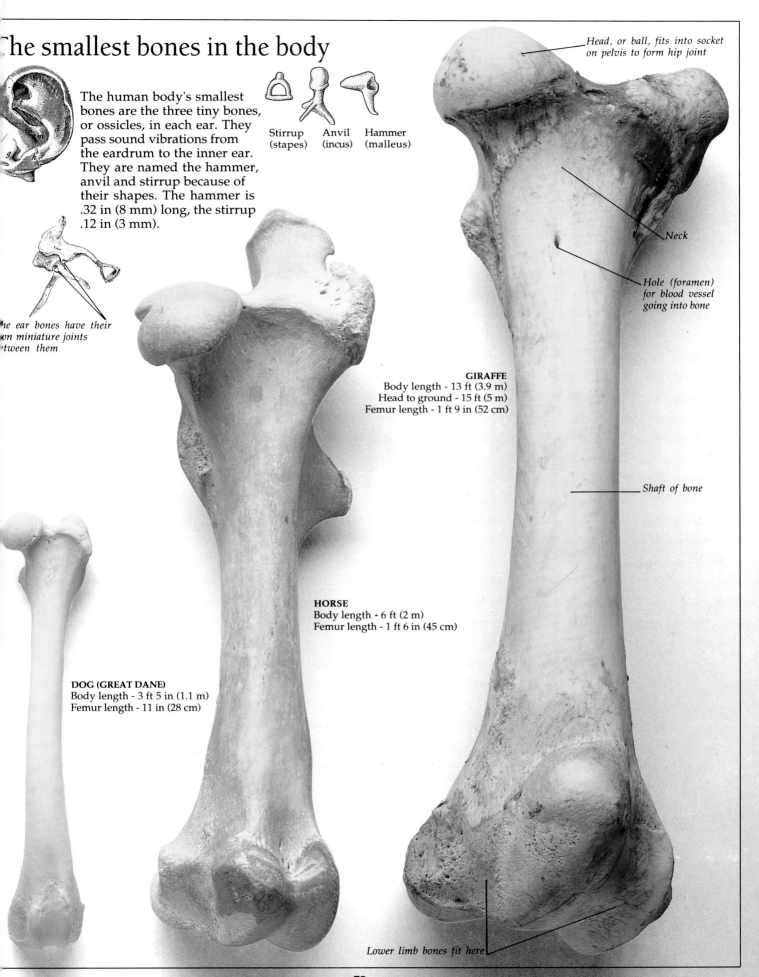

The smallest bones in the body

The human body's smallest bones are the three tiny bones, or ossicles, in each ear. They pass sound vibrations from the eardrum to the inner ear. They are named the hammer, anvil and stirrup because of their shapes. The hammer is .32 in (8 mm) long, the stirrup .12 in (3 mm).

Stirrup (stapes)   Anvil (incus)   Hammer (malleus)

The ear bones have their own miniature joints between them

Head, or ball, fits into socket on pelvis to form hip joint

Neck

Hole (foramen) for blood vessel going into bone

GIRAFFE
Body length - 13 ft (3.9 m)
Head to ground - 15 ft (5 m)
Femur length - 1 ft 9 in (52 cm)

Shaft of bone

HORSE
Body length - 6 ft (2 m)
Femur length - 1 ft 6 in (45 cm)

DOG (GREAT DANE)
Body length - 3 ft 5 in (1.1 m)
Femur length - 11 in (28 cm)

Lower limb bones fit here

Structure and repair of bones

LIVING BONES ARE NOT PALE, dry, and brittle, as they are in a museum case. Bone in the body is a busy living tissue. It is one-third water; it has blood vessels going in and out of it, supplying oxygen and nutrients and taking away wastes; certain bones contain marrow which produces blood cells; and bones have nerves that can feel pressure and pain. Bone is also a mineral store, containing calcium and other chemicals which give it hardness and rigidity. However, bone will give up its minerals in times of shortage, when other parts of the body (such as nerves) need them more. Bone tissue is made and maintained by several types of cells. Osteoblasts make new bone by hardening the protein collagen with minerals. Osteocytes maintain bone, passing nutrients and wastes back and forth between the blood and bone tissues. Osteoclasts destroy bone, releasing the minerals into the blood. All through life, bone is continually being reconstructed and reshaped as a result of the stresses, bends, and breaks it endures.

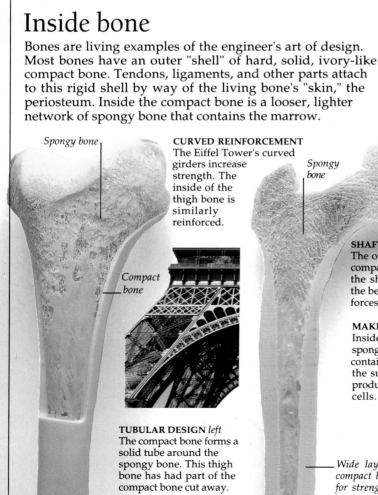

ISOTOPE SCAN
Radioactive isotopes concentrate in bone, and a scan shows their distribution in the skeleton.

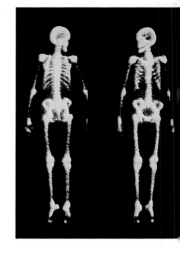

LIVING BONE
There are many ways of looking at living bones besides x-rays. By means of a pulsing crystal, this "scintigram" detects the concentrations of a radioactive isotope, which is injected into the body and taken up by bone tissue.

Inside bone

Bones are living examples of the engineer's art of design. Most bones have an outer "shell" of hard, solid, ivory-like compact bone. Tendons, ligaments, and other parts attach to this rigid shell by way of the living bone's "skin," the periosteum. Inside the compact bone is a looser, lighter network of spongy bone that contains the marrow.

Spongy bone

Compact bone

CURVED REINFORCEMENT
The Eiffel Tower's curved girders increase strength. The inside of the thigh bone is similarly reinforced.

Spongy bone

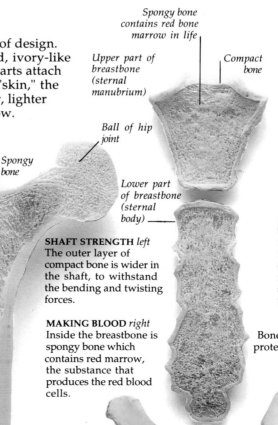

Spongy bone contains red bone marrow in life

Upper part of breastbone (sternal manubrium)

Compact bone

Ball of hip joint

Lower part of breastbone (sternal body)

SHAFT STRENGTH *left*
The outer layer of compact bone is wider in the shaft, to withstand the bending and twisting forces.

MAKING BLOOD *right*
Inside the breastbone is spongy bone which contains red marrow, the substance that produces the red blood cells.

UNDER THE MICROSCOPE
Spongy bone is made of a 3-D network of tiny rods, called trabeculae. Each rod is constructed of thin layers of bone plus the bone maintaining cells (osteocytes). The spaces between the rods are filled with jelly-like marrow.

BENDY BON
Bone is made of two main materials: th protein collagen, and minerals containin calcium and phosphorus. Dissolv away the hardening mineral (a week in an acid bat will do it) and th collagen is flexibl enough to ti in a kno

TUBULAR DESIGN *left*
The compact bone forms a solid tube around the spongy bone. This thigh bone has had part of the compact bone cut away.

Wide layer of compact bone for strength

Breaks and mends

Since bone is an active living tissue, it can usually mend itself after a crack or break (fracture). The gap is bridged first by fiber-like material, to form a scar or callus. Then bone-making cells (osteoblasts) gradually move into the callus and harden it into true bone. This is usually a little lumpy around the edges, so bone-destroying cells (osteoclasts) sculpt the bumps to produce a smooth mend.

FROM BREAK TO MEND
Broken bones mend mainly in response to stresses. A dog broke its two forearm bones (below). The main weight-bearing bone mended well; the other, which carried hardly any weight, never really knitted together.

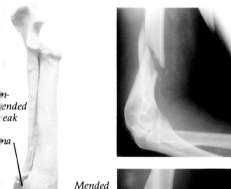

Un-mended break

ulna

Mended break on radius

ON THE MEND *right*
The x-rays show a broken humerus. It took several months to mend.

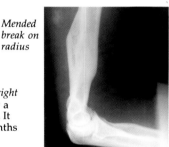

HELPING THE HEALING
Some broken bones need a "helping hand" to keep them in place, while the parts knit securely. In the past, a splint was the answer. Nowadays surgeons can use an "internal splint" - a plate of stainless steel screwed into place (below).

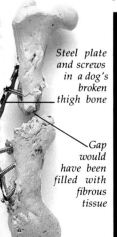

Steel plate and screws in a dog's broken thigh bone

Gap would have been filled with fibrous tissue

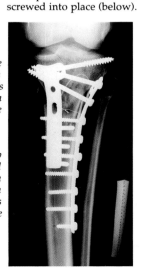

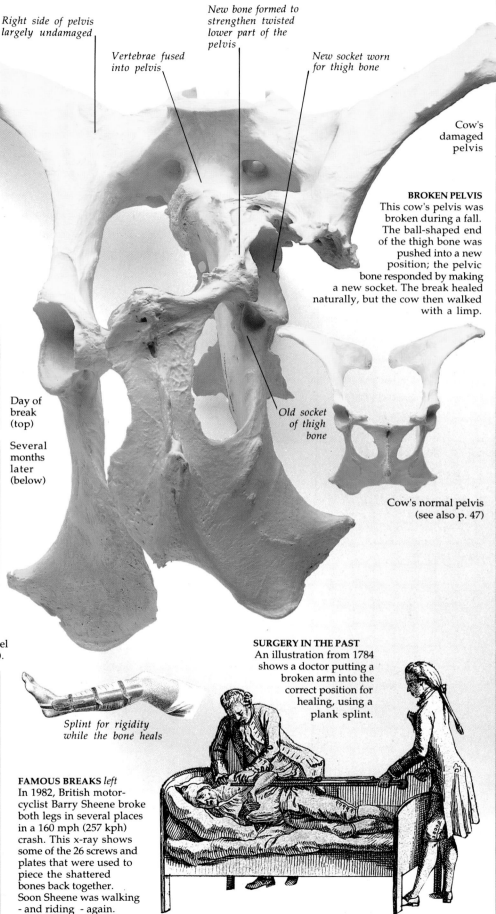

Right side of pelvis largely undamaged

Vertebrae fused into pelvis

New bone formed to strengthen twisted lower part of the pelvis

New socket worn for thigh bone

Cow's damaged pelvis

BROKEN PELVIS
This cow's pelvis was broken during a fall. The ball-shaped end of the thigh bone was pushed into a new position; the pelvic bone responded by making a new socket. The break healed naturally, but the cow then walked with a limp.

Day of break (top)

Several months later (below)

Old socket of thigh bone

Cow's normal pelvis
(see also p. 47)

Splint for rigidity while the bone heals

SURGERY IN THE PAST
An illustration from 1784 shows a doctor putting a broken arm into the correct position for healing, using a plank splint.

FAMOUS BREAKS *left*
In 1982, British motor-cyclist Barry Sheene broke both legs in several places in a 160 mph (257 kph) crash. This x-ray shows some of the 26 screws and plates that were used to piece the shattered bones back together. Soon Sheene was walking - and riding - again.

Glossary of bone names

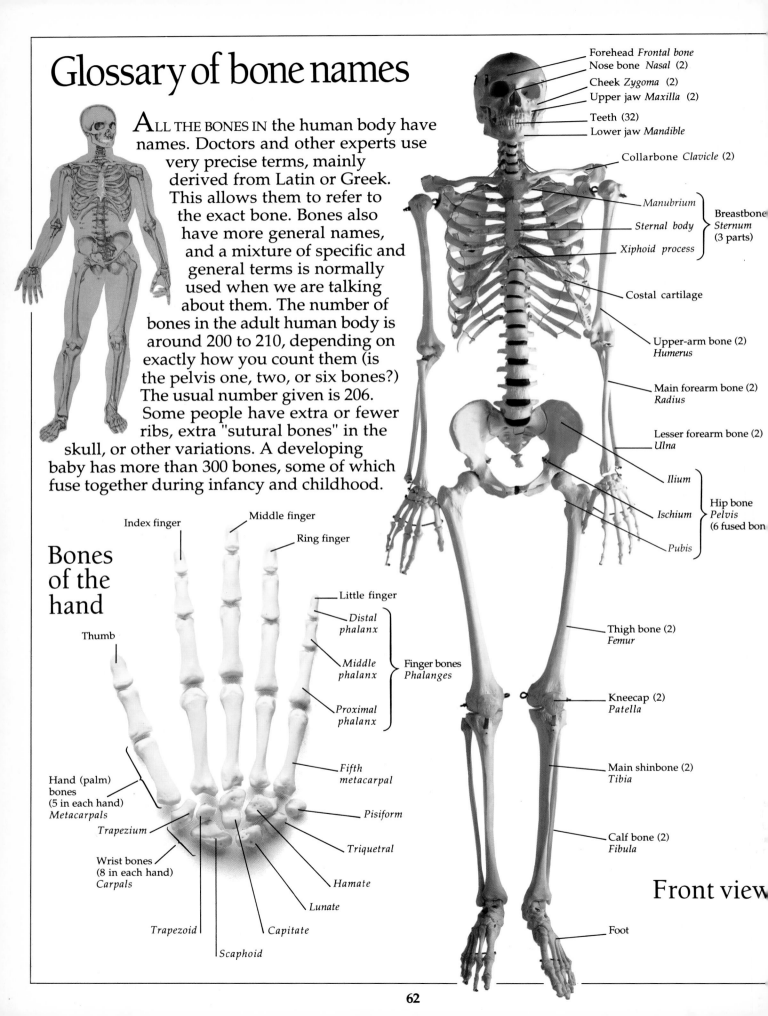

ALL THE BONES IN the human body have names. Doctors and other experts use very precise terms, mainly derived from Latin or Greek. This allows them to refer to the exact bone. Bones also have more general names, and a mixture of specific and general terms is normally used when we are talking about them. The number of bones in the adult human body is around 200 to 210, depending on exactly how you count them (is the pelvis one, two, or six bones?) The usual number given is 206. Some people have extra or fewer ribs, extra "sutural bones" in the skull, or other variations. A developing baby has more than 300 bones, some of which fuse together during infancy and childhood.

Forehead *Frontal bone*
Nose bone *Nasal* (2)
Cheek *Zygoma* (2)
Upper jaw *Maxilla* (2)
Teeth (32)
Lower jaw *Mandible*

Collarbone *Clavicle* (2)

Manubrium
Sternal body
Xiphoid process
Breastbone *Sternum* (3 parts)

Costal cartilage

Upper-arm bone (2) *Humerus*

Main forearm bone (2) *Radius*

Lesser forearm bone (2) *Ulna*

Ilium
Ischium
Pubis
Hip bone *Pelvis* (6 fused bon

Thigh bone (2) *Femur*

Kneecap (2) *Patella*

Main shinbone (2) *Tibia*

Calf bone (2) *Fibula*

Front view

Foot

Bones of the hand

Index finger
Middle finger
Ring finger
Little finger

Distal phalanx
Middle phalanx
Proximal phalanx
Finger bones *Phalanges*

Thumb

Fifth metacarpal

Hand (palm) bones (5 in each hand) *Metacarpals*

Pisiform

Trapezium

Triquetral

Wrist bones (8 in each hand) *Carpals*

Hamate

Lunate

Trapezoid

Capitate

Scaphoid

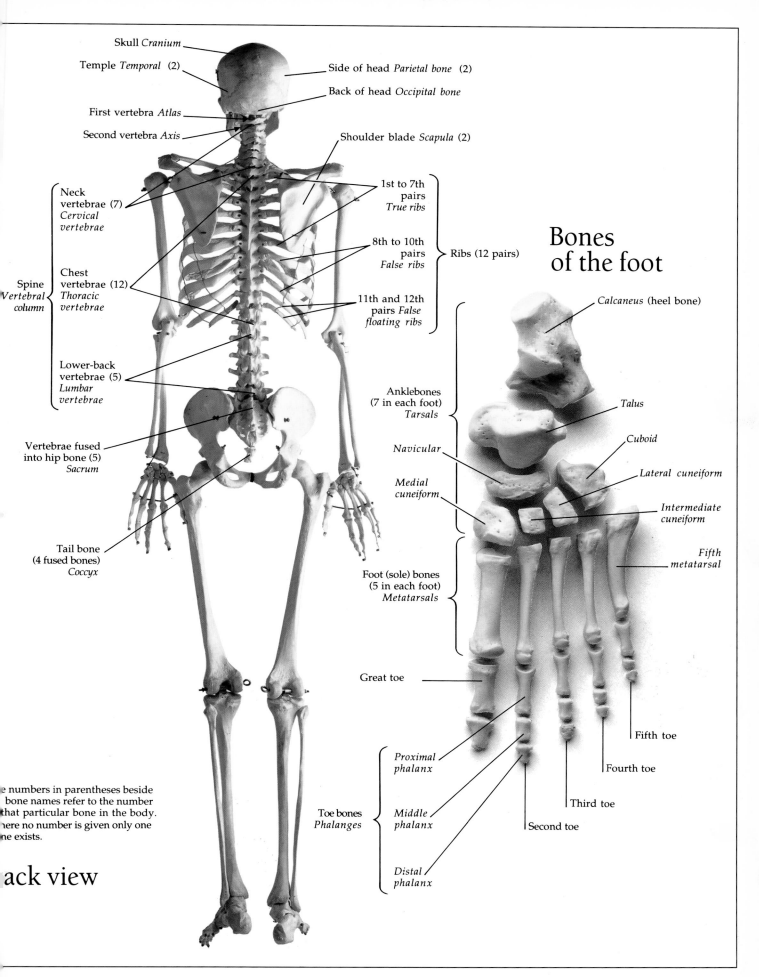

Skull *Cranium*

Temple *Temporal* (2)

Side of head *Parietal bone* (2)

Back of head *Occipital bone*

First vertebra *Atlas*

Second vertebra *Axis*

Shoulder blade *Scapula* (2)

Neck vertebrae (7) *Cervical vertebrae*

1st to 7th pairs *True ribs*

8th to 10th pairs *False ribs*

Ribs (12 pairs)

Spine *Vertebral column*

Chest vertebrae (12) *Thoracic vertebrae*

11th and 12th pairs *False floating ribs*

Bones of the foot

Calcaneus (heel bone)

Lower-back vertebrae (5) *Lumbar vertebrae*

Anklebones (7 in each foot) *Tarsals*

Talus

Navicular

Cuboid

Medial cuneiform

Lateral cuneiform

Vertebrae fused into hip bone (5) *Sacrum*

Intermediate cuneiform

Fifth metatarsal

Foot (sole) bones (5 in each foot) *Metatarsals*

Tail bone (4 fused bones) *Coccyx*

Great toe

Fifth toe

Fourth toe

Proximal phalanx

Third toe

e numbers in parentheses beside bone names refer to the number that particular bone in the body. here no number is given only one ne exists.

Toe bones *Phalanges*

Middle phalanx

Second toe

Distal phalanx

ack view

Did you know?

Pound for pound, bone is five times stronger than steel.

Compact bone is the second hardest material in the body. The hardest is tooth enamel.

People who are "double jointed" do not actually have extra joints, they just have looser ligaments.

Some people have extra tiny bones, called sesamoid bones, that grow within their tendons. These bones most often form in the hands and feet.

If a lizard loses its tail, it can grow a new one. In fact, the bones in a lizard's tail have special break points designed to fracture easily if the lizard is caught. The twitching, severed tail then distracts the predator, allowing the rest of the lizard to escape.

Three stages in the regrowth of a lizard's tail

Sharks, rays, and skates do not have any bones at all— their skeletons are made up entirely of cartilage.

When a person has a badly fractured bone that will not heal, surgeons can sometimes take bone chips from the pelvis and place them in the break. The chips grow to fill the gaps and heal the bone.

The axolotl, a type of salamander, is able to grow new legs and a new tail after a predator attack. It can even grow back some of its feathery external gills.

Some owls have ears on different levels. Each ear picks up a sound at a slightly different time, allowing pinpoint accuracy of the sound's direction.

The American Indian Blackfeet and Dakota tribes used to paint the skulls of buffalo and decorate them with sage and grass as part of their ritual Sun Dance.

The base of a coral reef is made up of the calcium-rich skeletal remains of millions of tiny coral animals. The longest reef in the world is the Great Barrier Reef in Australia, which stretches for about 1,250 miles (2,010 km).

Contrary to popular belief, men and women have exactly the same number of ribs.

When a child grows, bones such as the thighbone (femur) do not grow evenly from all points along their length. Instead, they grow only from the ends.

In a fall, a baby is less likely to break a bone than an adult. This is partly because a baby is lighter than an adult, but mostly it is because a baby's bones are not yet fully formed. A baby's skeleton has a lot of soft, flexible cartilage that will slowly turn into hard bone as the child grows.

Both sharks and crocodiles are continually growing sharp new teeth. When they catch prey, they often break or lose teeth, but new ones soon grow to replace them. A shark may grow more than 20,000 teeth in its lifetime.

Horn, a core of bone surrounded by horn protein (keratin)

A buffalo skull specially painted to be placed at an altar in the Blackfeet Sun Dance.

More than half the bones in a human are in the wrists, hands, ankles, and feet.

Horn is made up of many compressed hair fibers, and hair is made from the structural protein keratin, which also forms nails and feathers.

Around one fifth of a person's total body weight comes from just the bones and teeth.

Most people have 12 pairs of ribs, however, five percent of the population is born with one or more extra ribs. Some people, on the other hand, have only 11 pairs of ribs.

Orca (killer whale) skeleton

Chevrons, V-shaped bones where muscles join the backbone

An orca, or killer whale, swims using its powerful tail. Although it has no back legs, many whales do have a few vestigial (small, unused) leg bones, indicating that their ancestors once walked on land.

In order to avoid weak and brittle bones in older age, it is important to do weight-bearing exercise, such as walking, and to eat a healthy diet that includes plenty of calcium when you are young. Calcium-rich foods include milk, yogurt, broccoli, spinach, hard cheese, tofu, canned sardines, and salmon.

A cuttlefish "bone," such as those used by pet birds to sharpen their beaks, is in fact the living cuttlefish's internal shell. In addition to providing structural support, the shell helps the animal move around. The cuttlefish fills the tiny air spaces within the shell with gas to make itself rise, and then replaces the gas with fluid to make itself sink.

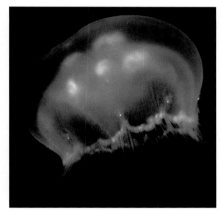

Jellyfish swim by expanding and contracting their bodies.

Some jellyfish can grow to 6 ft 6 in (2 m) long, and yet they have neither an external nor an internal skeleton—they get all the support they need from the surrounding seawater.

In the same way that humans lose their baby teeth as they grow up, young elephants lose their milk tusks when they are about one year old.

A single molar (grinding tooth) from an adult elephant weighs about 10 lb (4.5 kg). That's heavier than a brick.

Powerful jaws and strong teeth

By examining a skull, forensic scientists can work out what its owner may have looked like when alive. With use of either clay models or computer programs, they can build up the person's features based on the shapes of the bones. This method is used both to work out the identity of long-dead murder victims and to study people from ancient cultures.

Forensic scientists are now able to extract DNA, a chemical found in all body cells, from the skeleton of a murder victim. This can enable them to figure out the identity of a victim from just one small piece of bone or other tissue from any part of the body.

Fossil of *Sparnodus*, a fish that lived about 55 million years ago

The word "petrify" means to turn a once-living plant or animal into stone. Some fossils are formed when minerals dissolved in water flow into the gaps in buried bones, slowly strengthening the bone and turning it into solid, long-lasting rock.

Record Breakers

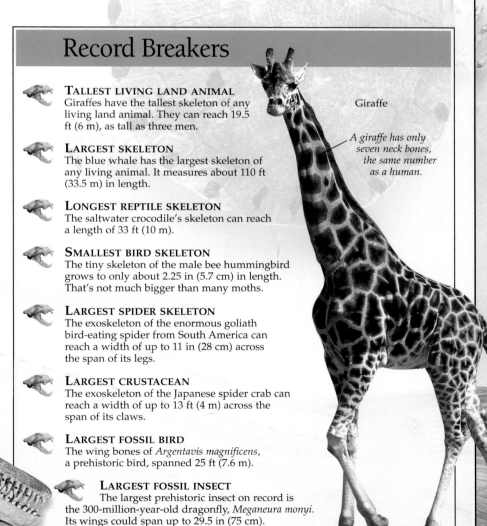

Giraffe

A giraffe has only seven neck bones, the same number as a human.

TALLEST LIVING LAND ANIMAL
Giraffes have the tallest skeleton of any living land animal. They can reach 19.5 ft (6 m), as tall as three men.

LARGEST SKELETON
The blue whale has the largest skeleton of any living animal. It measures about 110 ft (33.5 m) in length.

LONGEST REPTILE SKELETON
The saltwater crocodile's skeleton can reach a length of 33 ft (10 m).

SMALLEST BIRD SKELETON
The tiny skeleton of the male bee hummingbird grows to only about 2.25 in (5.7 cm) in length. That's not much bigger than many moths.

LARGEST SPIDER SKELETON
The exoskeleton of the enormous goliath bird-eating spider from South America can reach a width of up to 11 in (28 cm) across the span of its legs.

LARGEST CRUSTACEAN
The exoskeleton of the Japanese spider crab can reach a width of up to 13 ft (4 m) across the span of its claws.

LARGEST FOSSIL BIRD
The wing bones of *Argentavis magnificens*, a prehistoric bird, spanned 25 ft (7.6 m).

LARGEST FOSSIL INSECT
The largest prehistoric insect on record is the 300-million-year-old dragonfly, *Meganeura monyi*. Its wings could span up to 29.5 in (75 cm).

Did you know? (continued)

Q Why does a hermit crab live inside a mollusk shell?

A Unlike most crabs, the hermit crab does not have a hard outer shell on its abdomen. This makes it vulnerable to attack, so it lives inside an old mollusk shell for protection. As it grows larger, it discards its cramped shell for a larger one.

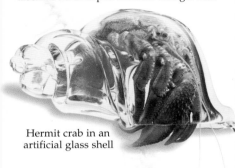

Hermit crab in an artificial glass shell

Q If bones don't bend, how can exercise make my body more flexible?

A Bones that meet at a joint are held in place by ligaments. Careful exercise can slowly stretch these ligaments, enabling the joints to have a greater range of movement.

Q Why doesn't a snake break its rib cage when it swallows a large animal whole?

A A snake has no breastbone. Instead the ribs are joined by flexible muscles. Also, the joints in a snake's backbone are very loose, allowing the body to coil and bend in all directions.

Q Why do cats' "knees" bend backward?

A The bones on a cat that are equivalent to a human's knees are high up near the abdomen. The joints that look like knees are actually the equivalent of our ankles, which is why they bend the other way. Cats usually walk on just their toes, which enables them to run very swiftly.

Q Why is regular exercise good for your bones?

A Exercise tones your muscles, enabling them to hold the bones in their correct positions, preventing health problems such as backache and bad posture. Regular weight-bearing exercise, such as walking or running, also improves your bone mass: It helps increase the amount of calcium stored in your bones.

Q How does an insect move its hard exoskeleton?

A The hard plates that make up an insect's exoskeleton meet at flexible joints. Muscles attached to the exoskeleton across the insides of these joints contract to produce movement; four different muscles pull each limb forward, backward, upward, and downward.

Q Do worms have a skeleton?

A A worm does not have bones or cartilage, but it does have what is known as a hydrostatic skeleton. Its body is divided into separate segments, or cavities, that are filled with fluid. The fluid fills out the worm's body in a similar way that tap water can fill a balloon.

Q How do huge whales manage to find and eat krill and other minute sea creatures?

A A baleen whale, such as a right whale or a humpback whale, does not have teeth. Instead, it has rows of fringed plates that hang inside its mouth and filter food from the seawater. Like human hair and nails, the plates are made of the protein keratin, although they are sometimes inaccurately referred to as "whalebone."

Q Do whales have tusks?

A Most whales don't have tusks, but the male narwhal whale, which lives in remote parts of the Arctic and sub-Arctic, usually has one very long spiraling ivory tusk that can reach as long as 8 ft (2.4 m). Some people believe that narwhal tusks washed up on the seashore may have given rise to the unicorn myth.

A hoverfly

Q Why does the hoverfly have black-and-yellow stripes like a wasp?

A Some harmless insects, such as the hoverfly, protect themselves by mimicking the appearance of dangerous ones. The stingless hoverfly's exoskeleton resembles that of a wasp so that predators, such as birds, will leave it alone.

Q How do x-ray machines see through skin to the bones?

A X-ray machines fire out a beam of invisible rays. These rays can travel straight through skin and other soft body tissue, but not bone. When a piece of photographic film is placed behind the body, the x-rays go through the soft tissue and expose the film, turning it a darker color. The denser bones act like a stencil, preventing the rays from reaching the film directly behind them. They leave behind a white unexposed image of the bones' shapes.

Spiraling tusk

Male narwhal whale

Q Do our bones have any other roles apart from supporting the body?

A Yes, both our red and white blood cells are made inside the bones. The red blood cells carry oxygen around the body, and the white ones destroy disease-causing organisms such as bacteria and viruses.

Q How does a spider molt its exoskeleton?

A Before each molt, a spider partially digests and absorbs the old exoskeleton, preserving minerals and starting to break it down. Lubricating fluid between the old and new cuticle then helps the spider shed the old skin, revealing the new one. The new skeleton stays soft for a short time, allowing the spider to grow.

Tarantula molt

Q Why do flatfish, such as flounder, have both their eyes on the same side of their head?

A The skeletons of flatfish have adapted to allow these animals to live on the seabed. Their flat shape prevents them from being seen by predators and prey alike. Both their eyes are on the upward-facing side of the body, and they also have a special cavity in their flat skeleton to allow for the heart and other organs.

Q Do animals with beaks have teeth?

A Birds do not have teeth as the weight of teeth would make their skeleton too heavy for flight. Some beaked marine animals, however, do have teeth. The common dolphin, for example, has about 50 pairs of teeth in its upper and lower jaws. It uses them to grip food, which it swallows whole.

Q Why are bones breakable?

A Because our bones are hollow, they break more easily than they would if they were solid all the way through. However, if our bones were solid, our skeleton would be too heavy for us to carry or move around.

Q Why do some animals have eyes that face forward, while other have eyes that point in opposite directions?

A Predatory animals (animals that hunt) often have two forward-facing eyes. This gives them a wide field of binocular vision, which is three-dimensional and enables them to pinpoint prey very accurately. Animals that are hunted, on the other hand, often have eyes that point in opposite directions. This enables them to look for danger all around and above themselves without needing to turn their heads.

Q Why are the exoskeletons of beetles and other insects so colorful?

A Often the only visible part of animals such as beetles and other insects is their exoskeleton. Some poisonous beetles are brightly colored to warm potential prey not to eat them. Other beetles are colored green or brown to blend in with surrounding plant matter and avoid being seen by predators.

Q What is the difference between tusks and teeth?

A There is no real difference: Tusks are teeth that project beyond the jaw. A walrus's tusks are elongated canine teeth, and an elephant's tusks are elongated incisors.

Q Is the part of a horse's hoof that we can see really its toe bone?

A No, the hoof surrounds and protects the fragile toe or finger bones. When the horse is alive, a pad of fat lies between the bones and the hoof to act as a shock absorber.

A horse's toe bones sit inside the hoof.

Sleeping parakeet

Q Why don't birds fall off their perches when they get tired or sleep?

A When a bird perches on a branch, it bends its legs and rests its weight on the bones in its feet. This pulls the leg tendons tight, clamping the toes around the branch. To release its grip, the bird must contract its toe muscles.

Male moose with antlers

Q What is the difference between horns and antlers?

A True horns are simple, unbranched structures that are never shed. They are composed of a bony core surrounded by a softer outer layer of horn protein (keratin). Horns are found on cattle, sheep, goats, and antelopes. Antlers, on the other hand, are branched structures that are shed and regrown. They are composed entirely of bone, and in life, they are covered with a furry, velvetlike skin. They are found on elk, including moose, and deer.

Find out more

IF YOU ARE INTERESTED in finding out more about skeletons, there are plenty of different ways you can do so. One of the most interesting options is to visit a museum. Most natural history museums are packed with skeletons of everything from spiders to dinosaurs. Many science museums have interactive exhibits that allow you to hold and investigate model bones, so you can see for yourself how they fit together and move. Some historical museums display the skeletons of ancient peoples, along with other artifacts such as clothing, household implements, and tools.

Other ways you can find out more about skeletons include searching the Internet and investigating the books, CD-ROMs, and videos at your local library. You might even want to find out about possible careers that involve working with bones, such as paleontology or physical therapy.

A PALEONTOLOGIST AT WORK
A paleontologist is a scientist who studies the bones of fossils, such as dinosaurs. Many paleontologists work in museums, where admission fees and grants help pay for their research. When museum visitors see a dinosaur on display, they are seeing the final results of years of planning and hard work.

MUSEUM
This museum technician is using a pair of callipers to measure the jaw of a bottle-nosed dolphin. The information she collects may be used to help construct models of the dolphin for display in the museum. Once her work is completed, the bones themselves may be put on display in the museum for visitors to view.

A physical therapist using a skeleton to help discuss a patient's condition

A *T. rex* skeleton at the American Museum of Natural History in New York

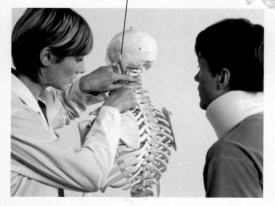

BONES AND MEDICINE
The first time many of us become aware of our bones is when we have a health problem. Physical therapists, doctors, and many other health-care professionals have studied the human skeleton in detail and can often answer any questions we have.

USEFUL WEB SITES

- A health-based site with information about the human skeleton:
  www.innerbody.com/htm/body.html

- A site that allows visitors to view, compare, and read about the bones of a human, a gorilla, and a baboon:
  www.eskeletons.org

- An interesting Web site featuring the largest *T. rex* ever found:
  www.fmnh.org/sue

- This Web site features short educational movies about bones:
  www.brainpop.com/health/skeletal

- A site about human and animal skeletons for young children:
  www.enchantedlearning.com/themes/skeleton.shtml

- An educational site with a fun quiz for older children:
  www.kidport.com/grade5/science/bodybones.htm

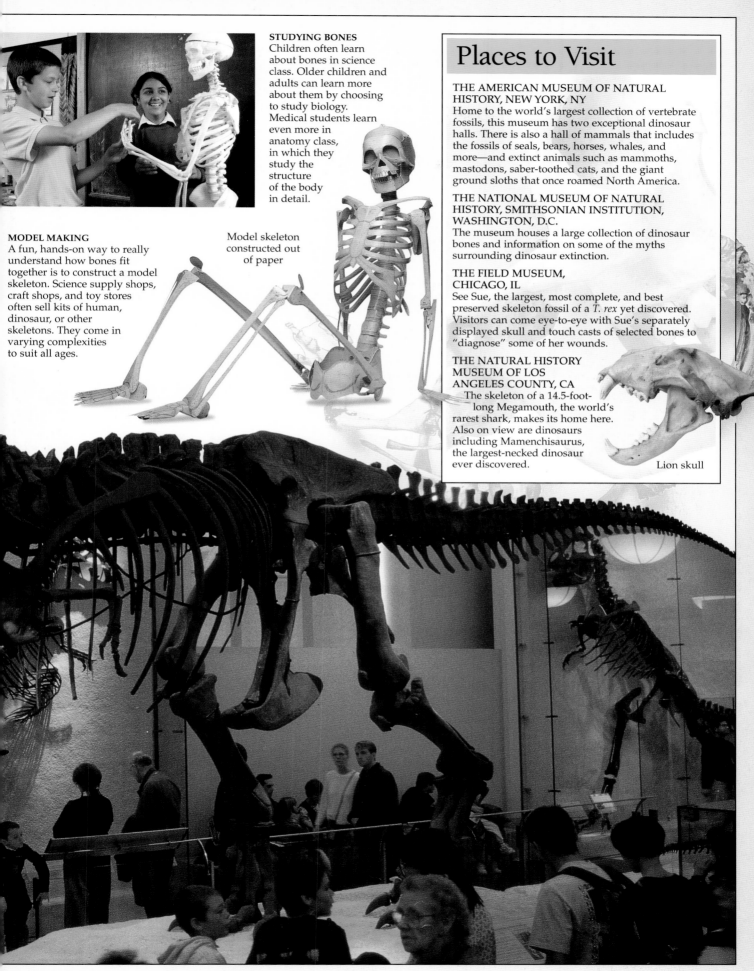

STUDYING BONES
Children often learn about bones in science class. Older children and adults can learn more about them by choosing to study biology. Medical students learn even more in anatomy class, in which they study the structure of the body in detail.

MODEL MAKING
A fun, hands-on way to really understand how bones fit together is to construct a model skeleton. Science supply shops, craft shops, and toy stores often sell kits of human, dinosaur, or other skeletons. They come in varying complexities to suit all ages.

Model skeleton constructed out of paper

Places to Visit

THE AMERICAN MUSEUM OF NATURAL HISTORY, NEW YORK, NY
Home to the world's largest collection of vertebrate fossils, this museum has two exceptional dinosaur halls. There is also a hall of mammals that includes the fossils of seals, bears, horses, whales, and more—and extinct animals such as mammoths, mastodons, saber-toothed cats, and the giant ground sloths that once roamed North America.

THE NATIONAL MUSEUM OF NATURAL HISTORY, SMITHSONIAN INSTITUTION, WASHINGTON, D.C.
The museum houses a large collection of dinosaur bones and information on some of the myths surrounding dinosaur extinction.

THE FIELD MUSEUM, CHICAGO, IL
See Sue, the largest, most complete, and best preserved skeleton fossil of a *T. rex* yet discovered. Visitors can come eye-to-eye with Sue's separately displayed skull and touch casts of selected bones to "diagnose" some of her wounds.

THE NATURAL HISTORY MUSEUM OF LOS ANGELES COUNTY, CA
The skeleton of a 14.5-foot-long Megamouth, the world's rarest shark, makes its home here. Also on view are dinosaurs including Mamenchisaurus, the largest-necked dinosaur ever discovered.

Lion skull

Glossary

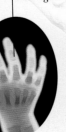

Human backbone

AMPHIBIAN
A member of a class of vertebrates that live both on land and in water, such as a frog

ARACHNID
A member of a class of arthropods with four pairs of legs, such as a spider or a scorpion

ARTHROPOD
A member of the arthropoda division of the animal kingdom. They have a segmented exoskeleton with jointed legs. Arachnids, insects, crustacea, millipedes, and centipedes are all examples of arthropods.

BACKBONE
A strong, flexible chain of bones that runs the length of the body in humans and many other animals. It is also known as the spine or vertebral column.

BONE
A hard body tissue that gives strength to the skeleton. In humans and many animals, it is composed of outer compact bone and inner spongy bone and bone marrow.

CANINE TOOTH
A pointed tooth, usually next to the incisors, that grips and pierces food

CARNASSIAL TOOTH
A specialized tooth on a carnivore that is adapted for tearing meat. Most carnassial teeth are large and long.

CARNIVORE
An animal that eats mainly meat

CARPAL
Vertebrate wrist bone

Hand x-rays showing the replacement of cartilage with bone as a person grows

Cartilage

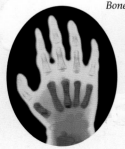

Bone

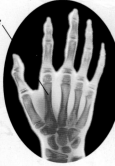

CARTILAGE
A tough, flexible substance that protects vertebrate joints. It is sometimes called gristle. Cartilaginous fish, such as sharks, have a skeleton made entirely of cartilage.

CHITIN
A light, strong substance found in the exoskeletons of arthropods

COLLAGEN
A connective protein that forms strong, elastic fibers. It is found found in bone and skin.

COMPACT BONE
The hard material that forms the outer layer of a bone

CRANIUM
The part of the skull that surrounds the brain

CRUSTACEAN
A member of a class of mainly aquatic arthropods, such as crab or lobster, with a hard case, or "crust," that encloses the body

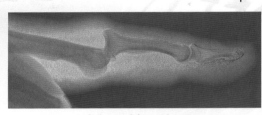

A dislocated finger bone

DENTINE
A hard substance beneath the enamel of vertebrate teeth. It is also known as ivory.

DISLOCATE
A movement that pulls or pushes a bone out of its place within a joint.

ECHINODERM
A marine invertebrate, such as a starfish, with a skeleton made up of hard, bony plates called ossicles

ENAMEL
A tough substance that forms the outer coating of vertebrate teeth

ENDOSKELETON
A hard skeleton found inside an animal's body

EXOSKELETON
A hard skeleton outside of an animal's body

FEMUR
Vertebrate thigh bone

FONTANEL
An area of cartilage in a baby's skull. It turns to bone as the baby grows.

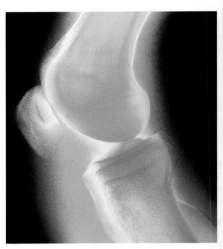

Artificially colored x-ray of knee joint

FORENSIC SCIENCE
The analysis of skeletal or other material in regard to questions of civil or criminal law

GEOLOGY
The science of the Earth's physical history and development

HERBIVORE
An animal that eats mainly plants

HYDROSTATIC SKELETON
An invertebrate skeleton maintained by the internal pressure of the body fluids

INCISOR
A chisel-shaped cutting tooth at the front of the mouth in vertebrates

INVERTEBRATE
An animal that does not have a backbone

JOINT
Any part of a skeleton where two or more bones meet

KERATIN
A structural protein that forms strong, flexible fibers, and makes up horn, hair, and nails

KNUCKLE
A joint between the bones in a finger or thumb

LIGAMENT
A strong, fibrous band of tissue that joins bones together at joints

MANDIBLE
A vertebrate's lower jaw, or the biting mouthpart of an arthropod

MARROW
A substance found within spongy bone. It is where blood cells are made.

MAXILLA
Vertebrate upper jaw, or arthropod mouthpart to rear of the mandible

MOLAR TOOTH
Chewing tooth at the back of a vertebrate jaw

MOLLUSK
An invertebrate with a soft body that is usually covered by a hard shell. The group includes snails, oysters, and scallops.

MOLT
The periodic shedding of an outer covering, such as an exoskeleton, fur, or feathers, to allow for growth or seasonal change

MUMMIFICATION
The process of drying and preserving either human or animal remains by natural or artificial means

NOCTURNAL
Active at night

OMNIVORE
An animal that eats both plant and other animal material

OPPOSABLE
An opposable thumb (in humans) or big toes (in chimps and some other animals) is one that can be manipulated to touch, or oppose, the other fingers or toes on the same hand or foot. This enables the limb to be used for holding and manipulating objects.

ORBIT
A bony socket in which the eyeball is situated

OSSICLE
Any small bone or other calcified structure, such as a plate in an echinoderm shell or an exoskeleton. In humans, it is used to refer to small bones within the ear.

— *Flexible caudal (tail) fin*

Pectoral fin

Vertebra

Cartilaginous dogfish skeleton

OSSIFICATION
The process whereby cartilage turns into hard bone. In humans, some ossification continues to occur after birth.

PERIOSTEUM
A thin, strong membrane that covers the surface of bones, except at the joints

PHALANGES
The bones of the fingers or toes in vertebrates, including humans

PREMOLAR
Vertebrate tooth that is situated in front of the molars

PRONOTUM
Protective head shield in some insect exoskeletons

REPTILE
A member of a class of vertebrates with scaly skin that lays sealed eggs. Snakes, lizards, and crocodiles are all reptiles.

RODENT
A member of an order of mammals with continuously growing incisors that are kept the right size by continuous gnawing. Rabbits and guinea pigs are both rodents.

SCAPULA
Vertebrate shoulder blade

SEDIMENT
Mineral or organic matter carried and deposited by water, wind, or ice

SEDIMENTARY ROCK
Rock formed from layers of sediment

SINUS
An air-filled hole in the skull. The sinuses around the nasal passages are filled with mucous-producing membranes.

SKELETON
A strong framework that supports the body and, in humans and some animals, provides attachment points for the muscles

SPINAL CORD
The cord of nerve tissue enclosed and protected by the spinal column (backbone). These nerves connect the brain to the rest of the body.

SPONGY BONE
A honeycomblike material in the interior of bones. It is filled with bone marrow.

STERNUM
Vertebrate breast bone

SUTURE
An immovable joint between the individual bones in the skull that helps provide a strong protective casing

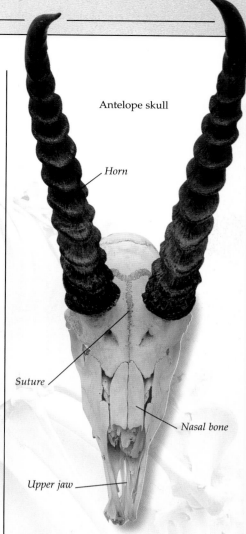

Antelope skull

Horn

Suture

Nasal bone

Upper jaw

TUSK
A vertebrate tooth that projects beyond the upper or lower jaw

VERTEBRA
One of the bones make up the spinal column (backbone)

VERTEBRATE
An animal with a bony or cartilaginous spinal column (backbone)

Image of a human scapula

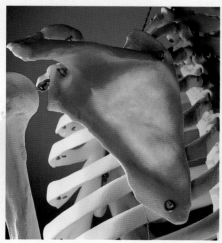

Index

Acknowledgments

The publisher would like to thank:

The Booth Museum of Natural History, Brighton, Peter Gardiner, Griffin and George, The Royal College of Surgeons of England, The Royal Veterinary College, and Paul Vos for skeletal material.

Dr. A.V. Mitchell for the x-rays.

Richard and Hilary Bird for the index.

Fred Ford and Mike Pilley of Radius Graphics, and Ray Owen and Nick Madren for artwork.

Anne-Marie Bulat for her work on the initial stages of the book.

Dave King for special photography on pages 14–20 and pages 32–3.

Picture credits
The publisher would like to thank the following for their kind permission to reproduce their images:

Position key: m=middle; b=bottom; l=left; r=right; t=top
American Museum of Natural History: 64tr.
Des and Jen Bartlett/Bruce Coleman Ltd: 51tl
Des and Jen Bartlett/Survival Anglia: 57b
Erwin and Peggy Baurer/Bruce Colema Ltd: 47t
BPCC/Aldus Archive: 9b, 10t, mr, br; 11t; 29b
Booth Museum of Natural History: 68 background.
Bridgeman Art Library: 8m; 9ml, 10ml; 11ml
Jane Burton/Bruce Coleman Ltd, 33m
A. Campbell/NHPA: 34b
CNRI/Science Photo Library: 26m; 49tr; 55br; 60tl
Bruce Coleman Ltd: 51br 67br.
A. Davies/NHPA: 34t
Elsdint/Science Photo Library: 60tl
Francisco Eriza/Bruce Coleman Ltd: 50b
FLPA - Images of nature:
Mark Newman 68-9b.
Jeff Foott/Survival Anglia: 50mr, 42m, 48m; 54m
John Freeman, London: 6bl; 7t;

Tom and Pam Gardener/Frank Lane Picture Agency: 33t
P. Boycolea/Alan Hutchinson Library: 11bl
Sonia Halliday Photographs: 43b
E. Hanumantha Rao/NHPA: 53b
Julian Hector/Planet Earth Pictures: 50t
T. Henshaw/Daily Telegraph Colour Library: 54br
Michael Holford: 9t; 11mr; 36t
Eric Hosking: 33br; 51bl; 42tr; 56m
F Jack Jackson/Planet Earth Pictures: 4l
Antony Joyce/Planet Earth Pictures, 33br
Gordon Langsbury/Bruce Coleman Ltd: 32tr
Michael Leach/NHPA: 56t
Mike Linley: 66tl
Lacz Lemoine/NHPA: 32mr
Mansell Collection: 6m; 7m; 15t; 36m; 43t; 56mr; 58t; 61br
Marineland/Frank Lane Picture Agency: 51m
Mary Evans Picture Libvrary: 6tl, br; 7b; 8t, b; 9mr; 10bl; 11br; 13br; 14l, r; 16ml; 26t; 45br; 58ml, mr; 62tl
Masterfile UK: 68bl; Dale Sanders 65cl.
Frieder Michler/Science Photo Library: 60m
Geoff Moon/Frank Lane Picture Agency: 32br
Alfred Pasieka/Bruce Coleman Ltd: 22t
Philip Perry/Frank Lane Picture Agency: 35t
The Natural History Museum, London: 66-7b, 68tr.
Oxford Scientific Films: Harold Taylor 66tr; M.A. Chappell 67tr.
Education Photos: 69tl.

Dieter and Mary Plage/Bruce Coleman Ltd: 40b
Hans Reinhard/Bruce Coleman Ltd: 32bl; 46bl
Leonard Lee Rue/Bruce Coleman Ltd: 32ml, 52ml
Keith Scholey/Planet Earth Pictures: 50ml
Johnathan Scott/Planet Earth Pictures: 37bl
Silvestris/Frank Lane Picture Agency: 35ml
Syndication International: 61bl
Science Photo Library:
68c, 70tr, 70c, 70bl; 71br.
Terry Whittaker/Frank Lane Picture Agency: 52bl
ZEFA: 37t; 39tr; 60b
Gunter Ziesler/Bruce Coleman Ltd: 37 br

Jacket images: Front: Corbis, b.

Illustrations by Will Giles: 12b; 13t, m; 27l, r; 28b; 29t, 34bl, m; 35tl, br; 37m; 38b, 39l, 52b; 44bl, bm, br; 45bl, bm; 46ml, mr, b; 47ml, mr, bl, m; 48ml, 49m; 51tr, 52m, b; 53t, ml, mr; 54bm; 55m; 56t; 59tm

Picture research by: Millie Trowbridge

All other images © Dorling Kindersley.
For further information see:
www.dkimages.com